MW00462407

THE WIDOWED ONES

Beyond the Battle of the Little Bighorn

CHRIS ENSS AND HOWARD KAZANJIAN

with Chris Kortlander

TWODOT®

GUILFORD, CONNECTICUT
HELENA, MONTANA

A · T W O D O T® · B O O K
An imprint of Globe Pequot, the trade division of
The Rowman & Littlefield Publishing Group, Inc.
4501 Forbes Blvd., Ste. 200
Lanham, MD 20706
www.rowman.com

Distributed by NATIONAL BOOK NETWORK

British Library Cataloguing in Publication Information available

Library of Congress Cataloging-in-Publication Data

Names: Enss, Chris, 1961– author. | Kazanjian, Howard, author. | Kortlander, Christopher, 1958– author.
Title: The widowed ones : beyond the Battle of the Little Bighorn / Chris Enss and Howard Kazanjian ; with Chris Kortlander.
Description: Guilford, Connecticut : TwoDot, [2022] | Includes bibliographical references and index.
Identifiers: LCCN 2021061383 (print) | LCCN 2021061384 (ebook) | ISBN 9781493045945 (cloth) | ISBN 9781493045952 (epub)
Subjects: LCSH: Little Bighorn, Battle of the, Mont., 1876—Miscellanea. | War widows—United States—Biography. | Custer, Elizabeth Bacon, 1842-1933—Friends and associates. | Officers' spouses—West (U.S.)—Biography.
Classification: LCC E83.876 E57 2022 (print) | LCC E83.876 (ebook) | DDC 973.8/2—dc23/eng/20220103
LC record available at https://lccn.loc.gov/2021061383
LC ebook record available at https://lccn.loc.gov/2021061384

♾️™ The paper used in this publication meets the minimum requirements of American National Standard for Information Sciences—Permanence of Paper for Printed Library Materials, ANSI/NISO Z39.48-1992.

CONTENTS

Acknowledgments

The preparation of this book has incurred many debts to respected librarians, historians, and archivists. We first want to thank Chris Kortlander for access to the rich collection of Elizabeth Custer material he possesses. It is his generosity that made much of this book possible.

The following are the other individuals and companies they work for that graciously provided primary source material:

Robert Lutey and staff at the Monroe County Museum and Monroe County Archives, Michigan;

The Little Big Horn Associates;

Steve Armour and staff at the Hargrett Rare Book & Manuscript Library, University of Georgia;

The US Military Academy Library;

Sharon Small, museum curator at the Little Bighorn Battlefield National Monument;

Moira Fitzgerald and staff at the Beinecke Rare Book & Manuscript Library, Yale University;

The staff at the Bancroft Library at the University of California, Berkeley;

Patrick Raftery and staff at the Westchester Historical Society, New York;

The staff at the State Historical Society of North Dakota;

The Denver Public Library;

Jane Woodman and staff at the Franklin County Historical Society, Pennsylvania;

Janene Crawford at the Santa Clara County Historical and Genealogical Society;

And finally, to Annie Yates's granddaughter, Suzanne Kelly.

INTRODUCTION

THERE WEREN'T MANY WOMEN IN THE LATE 1800S WHO HAD THE opportunity to accompany their husbands on adventures that were so exciting they seemed fictitious. Such was the case for the women married to the officers in General George Armstrong Custer's Seventh Cavalry. There were seven officers' wives. They were all good friends who traveled from post to post with one another, along with their spouses. Three of those wives were more closely bonded together than the other four. When their husbands were killed at the Battle of the Little Bighorn, however, all seven of the friends became, for a time, inseparable. One, driven mad with grief, eventually chose to separate herself from the others entirely.

Of the seven widows, Elizabeth Custer was the most well known. In the twelve years the Custers were together, Elizabeth lived history. She and her famous husband had been married a little more than a year when Lee surrendered to Grant at Appomattox and she was given the table at which the terms of surrender were drafted. After the Civil War, she and George traveled to various army posts across the American West. Trekking across the frontier was a thrilling chapter of Elizabeth's life, one that lasted until the memorable day when Custer and his comrades made their immortal stand against the Sioux Indians at the Battle of the Little Bighorn on June 25, 1876. During that last battle of Custer's men, Elizabeth was less than four hundred miles away at Fort Abraham Lincoln, waiting bravely for word of the outcome. Later, it was Elizabeth's duty to tell the officers' wives at the post that their husbands had been killed.

The public wept for the dead, and their hearts bled for the widows and young orphans of the fallen soldiers. Sympathy went out to all the women, but most especially to Custer's sister, Margaret Calhoun. Her husband, three brothers, and a nephew all perished in the same battle. For a time, a cloud that seemed to have no silver lining hung over the ladies' lives. Citizens insisted that one of the first duties of Congress should be to give each widow or mother of a deceased officer or soldier at least a year's pay, and give it without the customary haggling over the expense, as well as provide for her future wants by giving her a liberal pension.

The women were overwhelmed with letters of condolence. Most people were sincere in their expressions of sorrow over the widows' loss. Others were ghoulish souvenir hunters requesting articles of their husbands' clothing and personal weapons as keepsakes. The press was preoccupied with how the wives of the deceased officers were handling their grief. During the first year after the tragic event, reporters sought them out to learn how they were coping, what plans they had for the future, and what, if anything, they knew about the battle itself. The widows were able to soldier through the scrutiny because they had one another. They confided in each other, cried without apologizing, and discussed their desperate financial situations.

People throughout the country became possessed with a peculiar and dominant fascination with the widows of the officers who lost their lives at the Little Bighorn. Their husbands' deaths made their livelihoods dependent upon their own exertions. How they intended to support themselves and their children was of particular interest to many. The fight for woman's suffrage was in full force but decades away from being realized. Women weren't accepted at the polls nor were they considered for employment beyond that of a teacher, seamstress, or nurse. Some of the widows had no other choice but to move back home with their parents; one earned a living giving voice lessons, and another became a performer. Elizabeth found a job as a secretary and wrote best-selling books that chronicled her exploits with Custer.

In an interview Elizabeth did with a reporter for a New York newspaper in the spring of 1932, she was asked about her life as an officer's wife and the friendship she had with the other widows. "It seemed to me that we were always on the verge of some sort of danger, or else actually in the midst of the danger," she shared. "And yet we managed to enjoy life somehow. Life in camp with our friends and their families was never dull, I will say that much. There were so many dangers and so many hardships that we women came to be sort of fatalistic. That is, some of the women did. I was often worried myself, but I never really believed anything could happen to my husband so often did he triumph over odds."

The friendship the bereaved widows had with one another proved to be a critical source of support. The transition from being officers' wives living at various forts on the wild frontier to being single women with homes of their own was a difficult adjustment. Without one another to depend upon, the time might have been more of a struggle. *The Widowed Ones: Beyond the Battle of the Little Bighorn* is the story of how the women first met, the men they married, and how they persevered after the tragedy. "All dead? I still can't believe it possible," Nettie Smith, wife of First Lieutenant Algernon Smith, wrote Elizabeth in 1877. "If we mourn together the bitter pangs of loss, we will hopefully make it to the other side of our sorrow."

That's precisely what the widowed ones did.

CHAPTER ONE

God and Time Alone

THIRTY-FOUR-YEAR-OLD ELIZABETH BACON CUSTER FILED INTO THE Methodist church in Monroe, Michigan, on August 13, 1876, with hundreds of others attending the memorial service of her husband of twelve years, General George A. Custer, and five of his officers killed at the Battle of the Little Bighorn. She was adorned in a black bombazine (silk) dress with black fringe and a black bonnet with a black crepe veil. This mourning outfit would be her standard wardrobe for years to come. She walked mechanically, but purposefully, down the center aisle, her eyes focused on a reserved seat in the front pew. Friends and acquaintances smiled piteously at her as she passed; some refrained from looking at her at all. Those who knew of her and her well-known husband by reputation only stood on tiptoe and craned their necks to watch her every move.[1]

The heat that afternoon was sweltering. Members of the Baptist and Presbyterian churches had joined the Methodists to pay tribute to the slain soldiers who were raised in the town located on the western shores of Lake Erie. The combination of congregants along with the other funeral goers made the atmosphere in the house of worship oppressive. Halftones from the bright sun diffused through the stained-glass windows cast a colorful light on the portrait of General Custer sitting on the organ next to a magnificent podium in the very front, where the pastor delivered his weekly sermons. Custer's picture was surrounded with an evergreen wreath and two sabers crossed underneath the picture. The names of Captain Yates and Henry Armstrong Reed were scrawled across ribbons encompassing another display in evergreen.[2]

Elizabeth Bacon Custer

Elizabeth's attention was fixed on the national flag close to the lectern. She was quiet and composed. Her sister-in-law, Margaret "Maggie" Calhoun, was the opposite. She struggled to control her crying as she grieved the loss of her husband, Lieutenant James Calhoun; her three brothers, General George Custer, Captain Thomas Ward Custer, and Boston Custer; and her nephew, Henry Armstrong Reed. Anxiety was written in Annie Yates's every feature. Her husband, Captain George W. Yates, had also lost his life. More than a month had passed since Custer's Seventh Cavalry met their end at the hand of the Lakota Sioux, Northern Cheyenne, and Arapaho Indians in Montana Territory. The bodies of the widows' loved ones remained behind at the battle site.

The thought of continuing on before the men were properly laid to rest was overwhelming. Elizabeth and Annie had an easier time summoning the energy necessary to proceed with the memorial service than Maggie. In the days leading to the ceremony, Maggie had confided in Elizabeth how much she felt like "a nonentity." James had always boasted how necessary she was to his happiness. Now, apart from him, she believed she was nothing.[3]

Reverend D. Casler, Dr. Maltoon, E. J. Boyd, M. Venning, and D. P. Putnam all presided over the service. Each performed a portion of the duties. After the organist concluded the hymn "I Would Not Live Always," which Captain Thomas Custer had indicated that he wanted played at his funeral, Reverend Putnam read Scriptures and offered a prayer. Reverend D. Casler then read off the names of the departed.

General George Armstrong Custer, aged thirty-six, was born at New Rumley, Ohio, December 5, 1839.

Captain Thomas Ward Custer, aged thirty-one, was born at New Rumley, Ohio, March 14, 1844.

Captain George W. Yates, aged thirty-four, was born at Albany, New York, February 26, 1842.

Lieutenant James Calhoun, aged thirty, was born at Cincinnati, Ohio, August 24, 1845.

Boston Custer, aged twenty-five, was born at New Rumley, Ohio, October 31, 1850.

Harry Armstrong Reed, aged eighteen, was born at Monroe, Michigan, April 27, 1858.

Burial at Fort Leavenworth of the remains of the officers of the Seventh Cavalry, killed with General Custer
COURTESY OF THE LIBRARY OF CONGRESS, LC-USZ62-96104

"These names that we come to commemorate today no longer belong to private homes," Reverend Casler told the men, women, and children before him. "They are the heritage of the nation. They will live in history. When God's great chromometer shall strike the death knell of another hundred years, the name of Custer and his gallant comrades shall thrill the hearts of readers of history and be spoken with stirring eloquence from the lips of the orator. But while the glory of these names belongs to the nation, the great burden of sorrow belongs to private homes. If one of these heroes had fallen, we had felt like sitting beside the grief-stricken ones and mingling our tears with theirs; but how shall we utter fitting words when with one single blast a whole constellation goes out from a single home. The tender words of affection and sympathy seem harsh, and only silent tears seem eloquent today."[4]

At the conclusion of the two-hour service, those present at the event slowly filtered out of the building. A few returned to their homes, but many broke into smaller groups and huddled on the lawn and under trees surrounding the church. The widows left together, flanked on either side by extended family and friends there to support them in their time of sorrow. The bereaved wives were keenly aware how different their conditions were now compared to the start of spring. Their husbands—who had anticipated their every want, provided every luxury, and shielded them from every evil—were forever gone. Although the pain of loss would subside in time, what visions would they have in the days—and nights—to come of their spouses' slaying, their bodies' brutal dismemberment?[5]

Elizabeth held Maggie's arm as they proceeded past the funeral guests waiting outside the church. The weight of her sorrow was so heavy she could barely stand. Annie followed behind the two, using one of her husband's handkerchiefs to dry her face, which was wet with tears. The scene was reminiscent of the day they had left Fort Abraham Lincoln to return to Monroe, and back further still to the day they had learned Custer and his troops were dead.

Fort Abraham Lincoln, North Dakota, 1876
COURTESY OF THE LIBRARY OF CONGRESS, LC-USZ62-120167

Fort Abraham Lincoln, located at the point where the Missouri and Heart Rivers meet in southern North Dakota, was eerily quiet. The majority of soldiers stationed at the army post were gone. They'd marched away from the camp on May 17, 1876, with plans to return the following month. More than three weeks had passed since George Custer and his troops had departed with orders to intercept the Lakota Sioux and Northern Cheyenne Indians in the territory and force them back to the reservation, bringing about stability in the hills of Montana.

On July 6, 1876, Elizabeth was lying awake in her bed thinking of her husband and contemplating when she would see him next. It was almost two in the morning, and she hadn't been able to sleep the night before. It had been too hot to sleep. Even if the conditions for slumber had been more congenial, sleep still would have eluded her. The rumor that had swept through the fort around lunchtime greatly disturbed her, and, until it was confirmed, she doubted she'd be able to get a moment's rest.[6]

Elizabeth walked to the window and gazed out at the night sky, remembering the last time she had seen Custer and the Seventh Cavalry. The flags and pennants carried by the departing column had been flapping in the breeze, soldiers were waving proudly, and the horses had even seemed to be preening, showing how fine and fit they were. Custer had ridden to the top of the promontory and turned around, stood up in his stirrups and waved his hat, and then all had continued on their way. In a few seconds, they had disappeared—men, horses, ammunition, supplies, and flags—all on their way to the Little Bighorn.[7]

Over and over again she played out the events of the hot day that had made her so restless. Elizabeth, Annie Yates, Maggie Calhoun, and several other wives had been sitting inside her quarters singing hymns in the desperate hope the lyrics would comfort their longing hearts. All at once, they noticed a group of soldiers congregating and talking excitedly.[8] One of the Indian scouts, Horn Toad, ran to them and announced, "Custer killed. Whole command killed." The women stared back at Horn Toad in stunned silence.

Catherine Benteen, Captain Frederick Benteen's wife, asked the Indian how he knew Custer had been killed. He replied, "Speckled Cock, Indian Scout, just come. Rode many miles. Pony tired. Indian tired. Say Custer shoot himself at end. Say all dead."[9]

Elizabeth considered what one of the wives had reminded her about not putting much stock in hearsay. Their husbands had repeatedly reminded them not to believe any rumors. Elizabeth believed there might have been a skirmish but felt it unlikely that an entire command could be lost. At that moment, she had refused to believe Custer would ever dare die. She would wait for official confirmation before she did anything else.

Now, in her bedroom, listening to the chirping of the crickets and the howls of the coyotes, she sat up, wide awake, waiting.[10]

The loud sound of boots tromping across the path toward her front door gave her a start. She hurried to the door and threw it open. Captain William S. McCaskey entered her home, followed by the post surgeon, Dr. J. Middleton, and Lieutenant C. Gurley of the Sixth Infantry. Captain McCaskey held his hat in his hands.[11] He clearly didn't want to be there. Elizabeth looked at him, her eyes pleading. Just then Maggie

Calhoun and her niece Emma Reed arrived on the scene. The captain had instructed one of the enlisted men to escort the women to the Custers' home so he could deliver his news to the three women who would be most affected by it. They stood in breathless anticipation, hoping against hope their loved ones hadn't met with harm.

Captain McCaskey took a deep breath and reported, "None wounded, none missing, all dead."

Unable to move, Elizabeth stood frozen for a moment. Maggie was in hysterics. She dropped to her knees and sobbed uncontrollably. Emma threw her arms around her aunt and held her close.

"I'm sorry, Mrs. Custer," the captain sighed. "Do you need to sit down?"

Elizabeth blinked away her tears. "No," she replied. "What about the other wives?" she asked.

"We'll let them know of their husbands' fates," he assured her.

Despite the intense heat, Elizabeth was shivering. She picked up a nearby wrap and placed it around her shoulders. Her hands were shaking. "I'm coming with you," she said, choking back her tears. "As the wife of the post commander, it's my duty to go along with you when you tell the other . . . widows."

The captain didn't argue with the bereaved woman. He knew it would be pointless. It was common knowledge Elizabeth was as stubborn as General Custer, if not more so.[12]

She proceeded down the steps of the quarters to inform the other women of the tragedy. Captain McCaskey and Lieutenant Gurley followed her.

Still weeping, Maggie quickly got to her feet and hurried after the captain. "Is there no message for me?" she cried. "Did they have a message for me?" The devastating loss of all the men in her life was more than Maggie could bear. She collapsed onto the hard ground. Dr. Middleton and Emma hurried to her side, but she was too broken to move.[13]

Determined not to allow the agony to overtake her, Elizabeth continued with the grim task she believed was hers to perform. Without the other women to focus on, she, too, would have fallen apart. Her mind was fixed on being a comfort, while her heart thought only of how her life had ended with Custer's.

Elizabeth broke the tragic news to the officers' wives first. Among the women she visited in the early hours were Eliza Porter, wife of First Lieutenant James Ezekiel Porter; Annie Yates, wife of Captain George Yates; Nettie Bowen Smith, wife of First Lieutenant Algernon Smith; and Mary "Molly" McIntosh, wife of First Lieutenant Donald McIntosh. After the officers' wives, Elizabeth visited the wives of all the enlisted men and informed them of the tragedy. In addition to the women who had lost their spouses, more than sixty children had lost their fathers. By the time Elizabeth had completed her grim task, it was close to dawn.

In the days that followed, a cloud of extreme grief overtook Fort Abraham Lincoln. In between their tears over the outrageous loss, the widows struggled over what to do next. If their husbands' remains had been recovered, they were buried at the Little Bighorn battlefield. Until such time as the bodies could be moved, there would be no way to finalize their passing. The only thing that was certain was that the military would require them to move from the post.

Elizabeth had difficulty doing much more than rereading the letters Custer had sent her from the field. The last letter she received from him was dated June 22, 1876. "My Darling," Custer's letter began, "I have but a few moments to write as we start at twelve, and I have my hands full with preparations for the scout. Do not be anxious about me. You would be surprised how closely I obey your instructions about keeping with the column. I hope to have a good report to send you by the next mail. A success will start us all toward Lincoln."[14]

By early July 1876, word of what had transpired between the Seventh Cavalry and the Native Americans at the Little Bighorn had reached the public, from Washington, DC, to San Francisco, California. Numerous letters and telegrams of condolence were delivered to the Custers' quarters. Most of the letters of sympathy were written on mourning stationery—black-edged paper sent in black-edged envelopes.

According to custom, the thickness of the border indicated the social position of the deceased, his or her relationship to the letter writer, and the time that had elapsed since the death of the individual.[15] The majority of the stationery had thick, black borders—a tribute to Custer's rank and reputation.

Elizabeth spread the correspondence over every open surface in the parlor of her home, and there she stayed. She seldom ventured outside and ate just enough to give her strength to pore over the received messages. Many letters were from men who had served with Custer at various times in his career. Some were from Civil War veterans, friends and family, and others from individuals whose lives had been shaped by Custer's generosity.[16]

Colonel James Forsyth, a close friend of both Custer and Elizabeth's, penned a letter on July 12, 1876, from the Headquarters of the Military Division of the Missouri in Chicago, Illinois. "Filled as your heart is with the great calamity which has fallen upon you, in the loss of your beloved husband, I open this note with deep emotion," the colonel wrote. "I want to assure you of my heartfelt sympathy and to express to you my deep regret at the hollowness of these words to convey to you the depth of my feelings and the sincerity of my thoughts. Trusting that you will pardon this intrusion upon your sacred grief. I sign myself, Sincerely James Forsyth."[17]

"Dear Mrs. Custer," began the July 10, 1876, letter from Confederate Civil War general Beverly Holcombe Robertson, "While others with better claim have been sending you words of consolation, I have not ceased to think of and feel for you in this my serious dispensation of providence which has inflicted such a sudden and terrible blow upon us.

"If the tears of sympathy I had shed on your behalf could remove the sorrow of your stricken heart, I would consider them the sweetest obligation that could be placed upon the altar of friendship, but alas, I know how feeble and unavailing is any effort to ease your pain and to reconcile you to this cruel disease of Fate.

"Hoping you will receive the comfort of grace from a higher source and that we may all meet in a happier world, believe me. Your sympathetic friend, B. H. Robertson."[18]

"There will be many who offer you comfort and sympathy, in this your greatest trial of life," Lizzie Baliran wrote Elizabeth from Memphis, Tennessee, on July 15, 1876. Lizzie's husband Augustus had been killed by Lakota warriors in 1873 while on an expedition through Yellowstone. "But few who can, as I do now with my heart still bleeding for the loss of my poor husband under the same circumstances. I know what you feel. You have lost a noble man. I have much to remember and to teach my children of his great kindness to their father and to me a poor widow. Words cannot ease your grief now. God and time alone can do this. Only let me express my deepest sympathy. If I could relieve you how gladly would I do so. With many assurances of kindness from one who will cherish your husband's memory, as a great and good man. Believe me sincerely."[19]

Elliot Bates, Elizabeth's suitor from her school days, wrote to her on July 6, 1876. "My Dear Libbie, I do not believe there is anyone who can with propriety intrude upon your grief at the grimmest time as myself, and I cannot help sending this word of sympathy from one whose friendship you have known to be so true. My feelings for you and for the dear, gallant dead you know so well is sincere," Elliot shared. "The telegraph I received informed me that the Custer family died at the head of the column. Words are useless, and I will not attempt to say anything, for I know that to you there is but one consolation. You bear the most honored widowhood of any woman who has ever married a cavalry officer in this country. For George Armstrong Custer was the best of the cavalry officers we have ever had."[20]

Lieutenant General Phil Sheridan sent a letter, dated July 9, 1876, to Elizabeth that was meant for all the widows. "I take this opportunity to convey to you and to the ladies of the Seventh Cavalry who have been so deeply bereaved by the terrible loss you have sustained my sincere sympathy and condolences. And while conscious that nothing I can say will assuage your great sorrow, I can at least share in the grief you all feel. My acquaintance with General Custer and the officers who fell with him was most intimate, both officially and personally, and in a long service with those they sustained the high character now so justly appreciated by the army and the country for their gallantry and devotion to duty."[21]

While Elizabeth focused on her letters and telegrams, some of the other camp widows visited the post hospital. The day after the women were notified of the deaths of their loved ones, the steamship *Far West* had arrived carrying wounded soldiers from the battlefield. These men had been serving under Major Marcus Reno and Captain Frederick Benteen, two of the three battalions that had come under attack at the Little Bighorn. Benteen and Reno had ordered their men to retreat when they saw General Custer and his battalion overtaken, but the men had suffered injuries before and after those orders were given.[22]

The *Far West* had followed the Seventh Cavalry from the Yellowstone River to the Bighorn River with supplies for the troops. After the Seventh Cavalry's defeat at the hand of Sitting Bull and the other warring Native Americans, the *Far West* had traveled to the mouth of the Little Bighorn where she had been loaded with the wounded and dead. Captain Grant Marsh, pilot of the *Far West*, then drove the steamship to Fort Abraham Lincoln. The widows joined the wives of the men who had survived in hopes of getting details about their loved ones. They wanted to know how their spouses had died, what had happened to their bodies, and if there was any chance any of them had managed to get away. Some of the widows argued that in all the chaos a few soldiers might have escaped without injury. The widows were crushed when told the report Captain McCaskey had given them was correct.[23]

Elizabeth sent word to Captain Marsh that she and the other officers' widows would like to see him at General Custer's quarters. He knew they wanted him to describe the scene at what would eventually be called Custer's Last Stand. He declined the invitation because he "could not bear the thought of witnessing their grief."[24]

General Nelson A. Miles, one of the US Army's leaders in the campaign against the Native Americans in the West, sent Elizabeth a note in early July asking if he could visit her and convey his regret over her loss in person. The general and his wife, Mary, had been friends with the Custers for several years. Elizabeth assured the officer she would be honored to have him come to Fort Lincoln.

He was unprepared for what he saw when he arrived at the camp, and explained the scene in a letter to his wife. "You can have no idea of the gloom that overhangs that post with twenty-seven widows. I've never seen anything like it. Mrs. Custer is not strong, and I would not be surprised if she did not improve. She seemed so depressed and in such despair. What makes it more unfortunate, she has scarcely any relatives of her own."[25]

Elizabeth was alone. Born on April 8, 1842, an only child to Judge Daniel Bacon and Eleanor Sofia Bacon, her mother had died in 1854 and her father had passed in 1866. The judge had remarried, and Elizabeth's stepmother, Rhoda, was still alive. The two were close, but, apart from her, Elizabeth had no one. She was fond of her in-laws, Reverend Emanuel and Maria Custer, but, having lost three of their four sons, a grandson, and a son-in-law, they were overwhelmed with their own sorrow and unable to provide any comfort.

An article in the July 20, 1876, edition of the *Democrat and Chronicle* featured an interview with the grief-stricken in-laws. It was forwarded to Elizabeth at the North Dakota post.[26]

The reverend was sitting on the porch of the family home in Monroe, Michigan, when the reporter arrived for an interview, reading the first full account of the terrific struggle on the Little Bighorn River. "You already know all we know," the reverend told the journalist. "Have you any other sons?" the reporter asked after condolences were offered. "I have one other son who resides on a farm near here," the brokenhearted father responded. "Continuing the interview, Mr. Custer, while seeming reluctant to speak of the exploits of his sons, stated the following facts as to the three sons and the son-in-law who fell in the affair of last week," the *Democrat and Chronicle* article noted.

The reporter was kind, but made it clear he was interested mostly in George's background.[27]

They were all born in New Rumley, Harrison County, Ohio. George Armstrong Custer, known to his acquaintances always by his second name, Armstrong, was sent to the public schools from the time he was four years old until he reached his teens, when he came to Monroe and resided with a sister, and attended an academic institution here for a while, after which he returned and taught school in his native county, and also attended a select school at Hopedale. When about seventeen years of age, his anxiety to go into the army was such that he mentioned

Elizabeth Custer seated next to her husband, General Custer; her brother-in-law, Thomas Custer, is standing behind the pair.

it to his father in connection with a wish that he could get an appoint-
ment as a cadet at West Point.

"I thought it was a crazy notion," said the old gentleman, "for
Bingham [Republican representative of Ohio] wasn't of my party,
and I wouldn't think of his making the appointment."

But young Armstrong was in earnest, and he wrote a letter to
John A. Bingham, then in Washington, and gave such a history of
himself, his age, size, tastes and all, that his politics seem not to have
[been] thought of. At the earliest opportunity young Custer called
upon Mr. Bingham at his home in Cadiz and after some conversation
Bingham said, "Well, Custer, I think you will pass muster," and so,
not long after, the father was taken by surprise to learn his son had
actually received the appointment.

"Was your son here after his recent visit to Washington?" the reporter
inquired.

"He stopped here from the morning train until evening only."

"How did he appear to feel?"

"He seemed in as good spirits as ever."

"Did he seem to anticipate any trouble in the approaching war on
the Plains?"

"None at all. I remember he told me that Bloody Knife* had sent
him word warning Indians were going to take his scalp, and he laughed
as he said it."[28]

Elizabeth, Maggie, Annie, Eliza Porter, Nettie Smith, and Mary McIntosh assisted the widows of the enlisted men in packing their possessions
and doing whatever else was needed to facilitate the move from Fort
Abraham Lincoln. Replacements for Custer's column of the Seventh
Cavalry would be making their way to the post, and the families of the
fallen soldiers were to be on their way before the troops arrived. By the
end of July 1876, the enlisted men's widows were well on the way to having the wagons fully loaded with their belongings.

---

* An American Indian who served as scout and guide for the US Seventh Cavalry.

The officers' widows joined in with the same grim task at the homes they shared with their departed husbands. Most had been at Fort Abraham Lincoln for more than three years. They'd had ample time to transform their residences into showplaces. Now, removing pictures from walls, crating dishes, and packing heirlooms was devastating. To lose loved ones and a home in such a short span was more than women like Maggie Calhoun could bear. There were several times when Elizabeth would find her sister-in-law staring off into space, somewhat catatonic, too despondent to move.[29]

Elizabeth chose to have a portion of her household items shipped back to Monroe ahead of her leaving the post. Custer's desk and her mother's china and silver were among the items sent ahead. She decided to leave some of the furnishings and curtains behind for the post trader to sell to families en route to the post. In addition to determining what to do with the bedroom set, dining tables, and pots and pans, Elizabeth had to handle finding a home for the more than fifteen dogs (a mixture of foxhounds and staghounds) Custer had acquired during their time in the field. For help with that, she turned to one of Custer's friends whom he had met during the Civil War, Colonel Frank E. Howe. Howe was the managing director of the New England Soldiers' Relief Association. When asked, he agreed to take the animals, and, on July 27, 1876, Elizabeth had the dogs transported to the officer in New York. General Custer's dogs arrived safely late the following month.[30]

"Dear Mrs. Custer," Colonel Howe's letter dated August 29, 1876, began. "Have just come out of the woods—and only time to say that the dogs have reached New York and are in good hands. I have not seen them but will write you again about the 10th or 12th of September on my return. I hope you are better, and it would be a relief to hear from you. Your friend, Frank E. Howe."[31]

Another of Custer's possessions Elizabeth needed to manage was his favorite horse, Dandy. Custer had acquired Dandy while at Fort Leavenworth. Dandy was one of two horses Custer took with him to Montana. The animal was wounded at the Little Bighorn under the care of Private John Burkman in the vicinity of Marcus Reno's command, and had been returned to Fort Abraham Lincoln to recuperate. Elizabeth wanted her father-in-law to have Dandy. Lieutenant James M. Burns, quartermaster for the Seventeenth US Infantry at the post, took charge of making sure the animal was transported to Monroe.[32]

While Elizabeth and the other widows were preparing for their moves, additional reporters were swarming around the home of the Custer men. All were hoping for a statement about the charge circulating in Washington, DC, and in many newspapers that Custer's ego and desire for fame had placed his men in danger, men that would have blindly followed him anywhere, and ultimately cost them their lives.[33]

"They should not have said so," the distressed Reverend Custer stated. "I am his father, and shouldn't a father know the characteristics of his own son? He was neither proud nor vain. He fought to whip and not for praise. He was not reckless. He had much to live for, and he would not throw his life away. They shouldn't have said so."[34]

When newspapers carrying the reverend's comments reached the post, Elizabeth and the other widows were upset. The insinuation that Custer was impetuous and reckless and that those officers who served with him were incapable of independent thought was infuriating and disrespectful to the memory of their late husbands.

The officers' widows occasionally gathered on the porch of the Custers' home to discuss the way the press was reporting on the tragic event. Weeks after the battle, none of the women had been told the specifics of the deaths of their spouses. No military official who had that information considered it necessary to share. It was determined by the post commander that Eliza Porter did not need to know just yet that her husband James's body had been horribly mutilated and that his head had not been recovered. For the time, Grace Harrington, one of the officers' widows at Fort Rice, was spared the news that her husband Henry's body could not be identified and was presumed missing. Nettie Smith had no idea her husband Algernon had been wounded prior to the final battle on what would become known as Last Stand Hill. Molly McIntosh did not know her husband Donald was wrestled from his saddle and tomahawked to death, then dragged to the riverbank and scalped from forehead to neck. Maggie Calhoun and Annie Yates were unaware that the bodies of their husbands, James and George, were badly decomposed by the time they were buried in a shallow grave. Elizabeth had yet to know that Custer suffered several gunshot wounds, including one to the left temple.[35]

Eventually, all of the women would learn the horrific facts of their husbands' deaths. For the time being, they were content to prolong those specifics, although they had no tolerance for reports that blamed Custer for what transpired. The general's officers, their wives, and Elizabeth were a close-knit group. They trusted one another, revered Custer's leadership, and rejected all criticism of him.

On July 29, 1876, Elizabeth requested an audience with the widows and children of the enlisted men lost at the Battle of the Little Bighorn. She struggled to maintain her composure while waiting for all to gather on the steps of her home. The sound of little ones laughing and talking drew her attention away from her own hurt. She greeted the children and their mothers as they slowly arrived with a smile; when everyone had assembled, she thanked them for their friendship and loyalty and wished them well in their lives beyond Fort Abraham Lincoln. Before saying good-bye, she presented each child with a picture of General Custer.[36]

The following morning Elizabeth, Maggie, Nettie, and Annie, along with her three children, three-and-a-half-year-old George, twenty-two-month-old Bessie, and seven-month-old Milnor; Annie's brother, Richard Roberts (a civilian herder and part-time newspaper correspondent); and David Reed (Elizabeth's brother-in-law and father of Henry Reed) traveled to Bismarck, in the Dakota Territory, via carriage and steamboat. All the ladies were dressed in black, and all but Elizabeth were seen crying as the steamship carried the sorrowful party down the river.[37]

In Bismarck, the widows were met by Colonel J. W. Raymond and were guests overnight in his home. The next morning, they boarded a special railroad car to begin the long journey back to Monroe.[38]

The travels of the "widowed ones," a name given the women by the editor of the Minneapolis *Star Tribune*, were covered extensively by newspapers across the country. Reporters eager to get a glimpse of the forlorn women, especially Elizabeth, gathered at the train's first stop in St. Paul. They noted that they were able to see the widows through the window of the vehicle. "It is a tragic sight," an article in the August 4,

General George Armstrong Custer

1876, edition of the *Findlay Jeffersonian* read. "It is now thought that Mrs. Custer will not long survive her husband. Her condition is a critical one, and her death may be looked for at any time. The bullet that pierced the brave Custer was also the death wound for his loving wife."[39]

Before the train pulled out of the station in St. Paul the following day, another passenger boarded. Reverend Richard Wainwright had been asked by H. A. Town, superintendent of the Northern Pacific Railroad, which had provided the special car for the widows, to ride along with them and provide any comfort needed. Maggie Calhoun, in particular, was sick with grief, and nothing anyone did relieved her anguish for a single moment. Reverend Wainwright agreed to accompany the group until they reached their destination.[40]

When the train reached Fargo, where the passengers were to disembark for the evening, they found a large, respectful crowd waiting for them. All was quiet as the widows stepped off the train and walked by the solemn onlookers. Men removed their hats, and women and children lowered their heads. Stooped over and ashen-faced, Elizabeth led the way. She moved slowly as though the weight of overwhelming sadness had become almost too much to carry. As the last of the stricken widows passed the sea of townspeople, several citizens could be heard crying. Even the men expressed their sorrow for the unfortunate souls. They backhanded tears streaming down their faces or wiped their eyes with handkerchiefs.[41]

From Fargo, the mourners boarded the Chicago and Northwestern to continue their trip into Illinois. They arrived in Chicago on August 3. From the train station, the women were escorted by Colonel William Moore to a hotel known as the Palmer House. General Phil Sheridan had ordered the colonel to be there to welcome the widows to the city and to offer any assistance they might need.

Newspaper accounts of the widows' visit reported that, with the exception of Annie Yates, the distressed ladies were "very much prostrated." Had Annie not needed to watch over her three children, her head would have been down as well. Porter Palmer, owner of the Palmer House, and his wife, Bertha, offered their own private rooms to the widows and refused to charge them for their stay. The Palmers were so moved by the tragic event that brought about the loss of human life and the dignified manner in which the women comported themselves, they decided to start a fund to benefit the officers' wives. The Palmers contributed the first $250.[42]

Five days after leaving Fort Abraham Lincoln, Elizabeth and the other widows reached Monroe. When Elizabeth stepped off the train, all efforts to control her feelings abandoned her, and she burst into tears. Perhaps it was the relief of finally making it home after experiencing such unimaginable devastation. Maybe it was the memory of lost loves in such a familiar setting, or a combination of both. She had held herself strong for the others, but at that moment, she simply could not hold back her emotion any longer.[43]

Reverend Erasmus J. Boyd, longtime president of the Monroe Seminary and Elizabeth's teacher for many years, met the widows at the depot. When Elizabeth saw Reverend Boyd, she flung herself into his arms, weeping and then fainting. The reverend and other members of the church revived her, then led her to the clergyman's carriage.[44]

Maggie followed Elizabeth out of the train and was so overcome with emotion she could not make it down the steps on her own. David Reed and Richard Roberts helped her to the reverend's carriage and seated her beside Elizabeth. Annie Yates, her children, and Emma Reed exited the train last. Nettie Smith stayed on board. The trip would not end for her until she reached her parents' home in Herkimer, New York.[45]

Former first lieutenant Frank Commagere was present at the station when the widows' train stopped in Monroe. Commagere was a reporter who had been asked to cover the arrival of the bereaved for the *Toledo Journal*. In 1866, Commagere had been assigned to the Seventh Cavalry under then lieutenant colonel George Custer at Fort Riley, Kansas. During his time there, he had met Elizabeth and grown fond of both Mr. and Mrs. Custer. The editor of the *Toledo Journal* had tasked Commagere with interviewing the widows. Given his prior association with Elizabeth and witnessing the low state of health she was in, Commagere refused to question her or any of the other afflicted women.[46]

"[I] contented myself with the barren formality of a card par condolence," he wrote in the article, dated August 5, 1876. "Mrs. Calhoun, the sister of General George A. and Colonel Tom Custer, and widow of a third dead hero, Lieutenant Calhoun, is with Mrs. Custer, staying at General Custer's homestead, where the father and mother of the dead *sabreur* [cavalryman] have long kept the home fire burning.

"Mrs. Yates, the widow of Geo. A. Yates, who died in the massacre of June at the head of his company, is the daughter of Mr. W. Milner Roberts, engineer in chief of the Northern Pacific Railway, and a granddaughter of the late Chief Justice Gibson of Pennsylvania. [S]he had decided to establish her residence here, so that she may be near her loved companions in suffering, and has already rented a beautiful cottage on Monroe Street opposite the residence of David Reed."[47]

The widows spent the days after their arrival in Monroe visiting with family and close friends. They rejected unknown callers who felt compelled to stop by and pay their respects. Elizabeth warned Annie and Maggie against talking to strangers pretending to be concerned for their welfare, as some might be newspaper reporters hoping to get information about Custer's command by capitalizing on their vulnerability. Some publications continued to insinuate that General Custer's ego and recklessness contributed to the outcome at the Little Bighorn. The widows continued to be annoyed by the rumors. All found solace in reading the letters of condolence that continued to pour in from all parts of the country.[48]

Major General George B. McClellan, whom Custer had served under during the Civil War, wrote to Elizabeth in early August to offer words of comfort. "As a man, I mourn in your noble husband's death the loss of a warm, unselfish and devoted friend. As a soldier and a citizen, I lament the death of one of the most brilliant ornaments of the service and the nation, a most able and gallant soldier, a pure and noble gentleman. At my time of life, I can ill afford to lose such a soldier and such a citizen. It is some consolation to me, I cannot doubt it is to you, that he died as he had lived, a gallant gentleman, a true hero, fighting unflinchingly to the last desperate odds . . .

"My wife joins me in heartfelt sympathy . . . May God give you strength to bear under your burden of sorrow, teach you to look with calm resignation to the day when He permits you to rejoin him. Always your sincere friend, George B. McClellan."[49]

In a letter dated September 12, 1876, George G. Roberts, Annie Yates's brother, wrote to express his sorrow and share what life had been like at Fort Abraham Lincoln since Elizabeth and the other widows and children had departed.[50]

My Dear Mrs. Custer,

Mrs. Godfrey will write to Annie today, so I will mail a short letter to you, my kind friend. My thoughts are often with you and all the dear ones in Monroe. I look forward to my visit. [I] expect to fill Annie with so much pleasure, yet I dare not say for a reliable fact that I can get a leave.

No news in the post. Did I mention the new clubroom at the end of the lane? . . . It is almost finished.

The weather for ten days or more has been of the dark, rainy . . . unagreeable kind, yet I have not allowed it to tolerate any depressing feelings in me.

How can I say thank you to you at such a distance when I feel a great large thank-you always in my heart to you on the interest you have shown in my sister? I hope Maggie is doing better so that Annie can have more of her company. Annie can always tell you and Maggie anything that is in my letter.

Larry Milnore is sick. I hope he will be well again.

With kindness to you and Miss Emma Reed. Love to Maggie, hello to Annie and the children. You are all sorely missed.

George Roberts[51]

Neither Elizabeth, Maggie, nor Annie was in any state to respond to any letters. They were brokenhearted and lacked the will to do much more than make it through to the next day.

Maggie's grief had affected her physical health. She suffered with migraines and vertigo and spent most of her time in a quiet, dark room, seldom moving from her bed.

Annie kept herself busy with her children and tending to her home. Nights were especially hard. She shared with Elizabeth that she often imagined hearing George's voice calling her. She had trouble sleeping, and, when she did sleep, she dreamed she was back at Fort Abraham Lincoln, waiting for her husband to return.

Elizabeth transformed the room she occupied at her in-laws' home into a shrine to Custer. His desk with his books, papers, and journal was set up exactly as it looked at their quarters at Fort Abraham Lincoln. She hung the stuffed heads of the elk and deer Custer had hunted over the desk with his favorite pictures beside them. His uniforms were placed in the wardrobe next to her dresses.[52]

While the women were working through their grief, isolated from a world fixated on the Battle of the Little Bighorn, the editorial staff at the *Army and Navy Journal* was campaigning for funds being raised for a monument to those who fell with Custer to be redirected into a fund for the widows. "Many of the officers and soldiers of the Seventh Cavalry have left widows and little children behind who were entirely dependent upon the pay of their husbands for subsistence," an article in the July 15, 1876, edition of the *Army and Navy Journal* read. "With this prop taken away, they are helpless, or temporarily and gladly sheltered by sympathizing friends. . . . We do not mean to say that every one of the twenty-nine suddenly bereaved wives are in this desolate and destitute condition, but we are sadly aware that it applies to a large proportion."[53]

The response to the request in the article was overwhelming. Thousands of dollars were raised for the cause. T. F. Rodenbaugh, editor of the *Army and Navy Journal*, wrote Elizabeth to inform her of the money raised and to ask for a list of the widows and orphans so the funds could be distributed. She provided the information requested and asked that the portion of the share Maggie, Annie, and herself were to receive be given to the other widows. Months later after recognizing that Maggie and Annie were struggling financially, she sent a second letter.

"I wrote you some time ago that Mrs. Yates and Mrs. Calhoun and myself would be glad to have our share of the funds (so generously given for the benefit of the widows and orphans of those killed in battle) given the wives and children of the enlisted men. I, of course, have no change to make in my request for myself, but I want to ask you not to consider their request preferred through me. Both need the help and would gratefully accept it. I beg you will consider this letter as strictly confidential, for they do not know I intended writing and would object to my so doing. They are not needy but the change in their life is so great I do not see how they can ever learn to adapt themselves to the meager income they will have to submit to. The fund exceeds so far, all their ideas of what was expected be raised that I cannot think but that they would gladly accept the help and not feel others were being robbed of what they needed.[54]

"Again, begging you to regard my letter as a matter to be considered confidential in order to spare their feelings, I am sincerely yours, Libbie B. Custer."[55]

Elizabeth's affections and sympathy for the widows of the Seventh Cavalry helped pull her ever so slowly out of the pit of despair—a pit so deep her friends feared for her sanity. Contemplating the grief they shared gave her comfort. A tragic event had banded them together and formed the nexus of a friendship that would last for a lifetime.

CHAPTER TWO

Duty and Faithfulness

ELIZABETH CUSTER AND ANNIE YATES SAT ON THE FRONT PORCH OF the Yates home watching Annie's children playing in the yard. A stack of papers rested in the laps of both women, and when they weren't distracted by the unremarkable daily tasks of their new lives without their husbands, they sifted through the letters and government paperwork that had steadily arrived since late July 1876.

The summer of 1876 had passed slowly. The men who died at the Little Bighorn were sorely missed. Elizabeth had taken to sleeping with one of Custer's shirts. It smelled like him, and at night, when she longed to have him near, it helped to ease her pain. Annie spent evenings after the children were in bed writing letters to her deceased husband. She knew he was gone, but she had an overwhelming need to communicate with him about their little ones and the difficulty she was having, moving on. Elizabeth and Annie had found unique ways to deal with their grief and by mid-fall were venturing out into public, if only to visit one

Annie Yates
COURTESY OF SUZANNE KELLEY

another. Maggie Calhoun, on the other hand, still struggled, refusing to leave her parents' home even to attend church. "Now that Bubbie is gone," Maggie shared with Elizabeth about James Calhoun's death, "I do not feel that mentally I am fitted to fill any position of usefulness to others."[1]

Nettie Smith's correspondence to Elizabeth revealed her struggle to move on from the tragedy as well. "Last night I found a diary kept by Smithie on the Yellowstone Expedition [1873] in which so often he writes of his 'little wife.' In one place he says, 'These are hard marches, but it is consoling to know that we are marching toward my little wife Dudds [Algernon's nickname for Nettie]. God bless her! Only about a month separates us.' Oh, if that last part could only be true now. I realize the terrible truth more and more every day. Where shall we find the strength to endure?"[2]

Some of the other officers' widows weren't faring any better. In early October, Elizabeth had received a letter from Eliza Porter. Mrs. Porter had returned to Maine where she and her husband James had met and married. She wanted her two sons to be near her family in Franklin County. The Porters' first child, David, had been born in 1871 in Massachusetts, and their second boy, James, had been born in March 1876 at Fort Abraham Lincoln. Elizabeth had been with her at the birth.[3]

"I regret so much that I could not have written you sooner," Eliza noted in her letter to Elizabeth, dated September 18, 1876. "My boys are all I have left of James. I have been lost without him. After arriving home to Strong [Maine], I did not have a moment to let you know of my whereabouts. Preparing for the tedious and burdensome journey here was all consuming. I have thought since that time it was better that we endured the trip than to have stayed behind hoping James's body would eventually be recovered."[4]

In addition to dealing with the great loss they'd all experienced, the widows of the officers were angst-ridden over how to cope financially in the long term. In July 1876, the House of Representatives had passed a bill granting a $50 a month pension for Elizabeth. All the women whose husbands had died at the Little Bighorn would receive a pension based on the men's rank and the children they had. General Custer, Captain

Yates, Lieutenant Calhoun, and First Lieutenant Porter all had life insurance policies with New York Life Insurance, and, by the end of the summer, the widows had received settlements from the company. Elizabeth, Annie, Maggie, and Eliza were given a $5,000 payout. The relief fund sponsored by the *Army and Navy Journal* eventually provided all the widows, officer and enlisted alike, with additional funds.[5]

When Annie's youngest child started crying, she left the porch to collect the children and take them inside for their naps. Like Eliza Porter's youngest son, Annie's little boy Milnor had been born at Fort Abraham Lincoln, and, like Eliza, Elizabeth was by her friend's side when the blessed event had occurred. While waiting for Annie to return, Elizabeth turned her attention to a letter she had received from Captain Myles Moylan. The captain had fought with the Seventh Cavalry at the Battle of the Little Bighorn as the commander of Company A under Major Marcus Reno. He was married to Charlotte Calhoun, Lieutenant James Calhoun's sister and Maggie Custer Calhoun's sister-in-law. The October 3, 1876, letter he penned to Elizabeth was sent from Fort Abraham Lincoln.[6]

My Dear, Mrs. Custer,

Do not think it strange that I have allowed so long a time to elaps [sic] since that terrible day when you lost so many that were so dear to you and when I lost the best friend I ever had, without writing you. I have often tried to do so several times but have failed every time; before commencing I can think of a thousand things to say, but when I tried to commit them to paper, they all forsook me; nothing remained but that one thing, that horrible fact that he was gone.

You will not think hard of me for not attending to this duty sooner, for if ever a man owed a duty and faithfulness, I do to the widow of the man who from the beginning to the end was to me the best friend man ever had.

I cannot write of what I saw on the 27th of June when we went over the field and buried the dead. It is unnecessary for me to say who the noble men were who were true to him at the last. There were the men of his own blood lying around him. There also was the noble

Cooke, Yates, and Smith all lying close by the leader they all honored and loved so well. Some distance in front was the cold clay of a gallant man as ever lived—our Jim. I cannot say anymore.

A day will come, and thank God it is not far distant, when Justice will be done for the dead of the Little Bighorn. Who could have foreseen such misfortune? I hope to see you this winter sometime; we expect to go east as soon as I [can] get away. Lottie [sends] love to yourself and our other friends.

God bless you forever shall ever be the prayer of the men to whom in the goodness of your heart you have ever shown so much kindness. Again, I say, from my heart, God bless you.

> *Your sincere friend,*
> *M. Moylan.*[7]

Elizabeth pondered Captain Moylan's question, "Who could have foreseen such misfortune?" She recalled the day when she and Custer had first arrived at Fort Abraham Lincoln in November 1873. The bulk of Custer's Seventh Cavalry Regiment, along with their wives and children, were already situated at the Dakota Territory's military post. Annie and George Yates were among the group of close friends who regularly congregated around Custer and Elizabeth. The two Georges had met during the Civil War, and Annie had been brought into the fold in the summer of 1870 after a visit to Fort Hays, at the request of her uncle, Major George Gibson. During Annie's stay at the fort, she met her future husband.

George Wilhelmus Mancius "Walter" Yates was a twenty-seven-year-old captain from Albany, New York, who enjoyed buffalo hunting. Twenty-one-year-old Annie Gibson Roberts accompanied General Custer, his staff, of which George was a part, and a few other brave women, including Elizabeth, on a buffalo-hunting expedition in early July 1870. Annie and George Yates rode together on a large gray horse named Badger. The couple bonded over their mutual love for horses and adventure and the beauty of the Kansas plains.[8]

"A background of graceful hill-slopes covered with odorous buffalo grass, and the rich coloring of the carpet naturally formed by it and var-

George Yates
COURTESY OF THE NATIONAL PARK SERVICE, LITTLE
BIGHORN BATTLEFIELD NATIONAL MONUMENT

iegated with flowers of every hue, at my feet made a charming scene," Annie recalled in her journal. "Never do I expect to see such a sight again. Over 10,000 buffalo running over the prairie. It was like going into battle, so the officers said. If the country had not been so broken up, we should have chased better. However, I was on Captain Yates'[s] horse, not afraid of buffalo, and we fairly flew over the ground."[9]

Annie was smitten with George and described him as a man with a "perfectly proportioned" physique. In her words, "He was 5 feet 11 inches in height, weighing one hundred and eighty-six pounds; his eyes of a deep blue were very keen and observant; his blond complexion and beautiful, fine golden hair and long moustache were bronzed by much exposure though his cheeks still showed every emotion."[10]

George and Annie saw a lot of one another during her time at Fort Hays, and when she returned to her parents' home in Philadelphia, the two corresponded. Annie's father, Milnor Roberts, put a stop to his daughter exchanging letters with George based in part on the fact that

The Custers, his officers, and their wives enjoyed many outings together, such as this one near Fort Hays, Kansas.
COURTESY OF THE NATIONAL PARK SERVICE, LITTLE BIGHORN BATTLEFIELD NATIONAL MONUMENT, LIBI_00019_00498, PHOTOGRAPHED BY W. J. PHILLIPS, CIRCA 1869

George had been married and divorced. It took the combined effort of her brother, Elizabeth, Custer, and her other friends to convince Milnor that Captain Yates was a respectable individual.[11]

Annie and George were married on February 12, 1872, at St. George's Episcopal Church in Manhattan. The following day, the couple traveled to Kentucky where his Seventh Cavalry company was ordered to report. Annie adapted to military life quickly. Her natural charm and sense of humor contributed to her popularity among the other wives of the Seventh Cavalry.[12]

Their first son, George Livingston, was born on December 11, 1872, in Louisville, Kentucky. Custer wrote Elizabeth about the news of the birth on February 9, 1873. "Annie Yates has had a baby, but it is barefooted on top of its head, like some other member of the family." Custer was referring to the infant's father, whose hair was noticeably thinning.[13]

By April 1873, the Yates family was living at Fort Rice in the Dakota Territory. Troops had been dispatched to the post to protect an expedition of surveyors and engineers with the Northern Pacific Railroad who were working to extend the rail line between the Missouri River and the Rocky Mountains.[14]

The trip to the northern plains' outpost west of the upper Missouri River was grueling for Annie. She would have to make the trip alone, as George was needed for reconnaissance work on horseback with a regiment of troops. She traveled by steamship on the Ohio River from Louisville to Cairo, Illinois, then boarded a train that transported mother and child to Yankton, Dakota, where Annie and the other dependents and soldiers were overtaken by a blizzard.

When the weather cleared, the sojourners were ushered onto a steamship called the *Minor*. A shaft broke on the steamer midway to its destination, and the craft had to dock for repairs while passengers remained on board. Annie got sick from exposure to the frigid winds blowing across the cold water. According to Second Lieutenant Charles Larned, one of the soldiers on the journey, Annie's condition was serious. "Poor woman," he wrote in a letter to his mother. "She had a chill every other day on the way up and is emaciated almost to a skeleton. Her baby wears her out and the drain on her constitution in nursing it has been very severe."[15]

As Yates had already departed on the expedition on which the army had ordered him and the other members of the Seventh Cavalry to participate, he could not leave to get to his ill wife and baby. Annie's father and brother, John, met mother and infant in Bismarck and escorted the two to John's home in Wisconsin. Annie and little George remained there until George was close to returning home from his mission and was stationed at Fort Abraham Lincoln.[16]

Captain Yates received a letter from his wife in late June explaining what had happened. He was despondent over Annie's fragile health and dealt with the frustration of not being able to be with her by drinking and playing cards. His behavior wasn't consistent with how he usually acted, and it prompted Custer and some of his other friends to intercede. Custer wrote Elizabeth about the situation, lamenting that Captain Yates would be a "confirmed drunkard" if he continued on this course. He added that he saw "but little happiness for his poor wife," if things didn't change. Elizabeth's response expressed her concern over the matter.[17]

"She [Maggie] and I are perfectly despondent about Captain Z* [Yates]," Elizabeth wrote Custer in July 1873. "Do, Autie, write him a strong letter, reminding him how she [Annie] proved her love by marrying him in the face of family opposition. Now, Autie, we must redouble our efforts to befriend her, sweet sensitive soul that she is."[18]

Captain Yates and the other soldiers with the Seventh Cavalry concluded their expedition in early fall 1873 and arrived at Fort Abraham Lincoln on September 23. Annie and their little boy were there to meet him at the post. The pair had arrived at the fort in mid-August. Annie and George were happy to be together again, and life at the military post was exciting.

The news of the activities at Fort Abraham Lincoln appeared in the September 11, 1873, edition of the *Helena Weekly Herald*:[19]

> *A schoolhouse is being built at Lincoln in order to give school facilities to the children of the officers, soldiers, and citizens. There are about twenty to thirty of the little fellows to look after. A teacher has been engaged from St. Paul.*
>
> *General Custer will have command of the Cavalry Barracks, near Fort Lincoln. Six companies of the Seventh Cavalry will be stationed there, four at Fort Rice and two at Fort Totten. The head-quarters of the regiment will probably be at Totten.*
>
> *The carpenters at the cavalry barracks, near Fort Lincoln, have determined to issue a little weekly paper, devoted to their mutual interests and improvement, C. H. Townsend, editor. The paper will be out Saturday next, and then the* Tribune *can no longer boast of being published the farthest west, for the* Mechanics Far West *will beat it [by] four miles.*[20]

When George wasn't busy with his regular duties as a soldier and Annie wasn't busy with the baby and fulfilling her civic obligations, the couple spent time at the Custers' quarters, socializing with the other officers and their wives who were part of Custer's group of close friends.[21]

---

* Captain Z is the name Custer used to refer to George Yates in his letter to Elizabeth.

The Custers' quarters at Fort Lincoln, North Dakota, 1875
COURTESY OF THE STATE HISTORICAL SOCIETY OF NORTH DAKOTA, B0129-00001

On July 2, 1874, Annie and George were once again separated as the Seventh Cavalry left Fort Abraham Lincoln to embark on an expedition to the Dakota Territory's Black Hills. Ten companies of the Seventh, three companies of infantry, one hundred Indian scouts, and a battery of Gatling guns all under the command of General Custer set out on a three-month trek to explore the legendary region for the purposes of establishing a site for the building of a fort and trading post.[22]

Annie and the wives left behind at Fort Abraham Lincoln were anxious about their husbands traveling to the Black Hills. Rumor had it that the Sioux tribes were mounting a strong resistance to the military infiltration. An Indian missionary who visited Fort Abraham Lincoln in late June 1874 reported that the Sioux "intended to contest every foot of the march," and he pleaded with Custer to give up the expedition to avoid bloodshed. Custer refused and noted that the treaty the United States government had with the Sioux gave the army the right to pass through and explore all the contested territory. Custer promised to enforce that right. The missionary predicted a major battle could be expected in the near future.[23]

When George left Annie to follow Custer's command, she was seven months pregnant with their second child. George wrote his wife as often as he could and on whatever paper was available. On one occasion, he scrawled a note to Annie on government-issued toilet paper.[24]

My Dear Annie,

I take up my pen to write you a few lines to let you know that I am well and so hope that you are the same. I have not much time to write, Love, but I believe you would think I am not a very affectionate husband if I did not send just one word. I have already told you much about our trip, and I will only add now that it has been one of the pleasantest trips I ever enjoyed. Words fail me to describe the beauties of the lovely valleys through which we have passed—especially Floral Valley, walled in by high hills, traversed by pure streams and perfectly exuberant with flowers, plenty of good water, almost as cold as ice, abundant shade, fine grass, plenty of game, raspberries, strawberries, gooseberries, June berries (Amelanchier) are some of the delights of this region. The scenery, too, is beautiful. But you will learn more of particulars by reading Mr. Barrows'[s] letter in the Tribune.

I hope you are enjoying yourself at Lincoln and that you are not pining away on my account. I will only be a few days, Dearie, before I again clasp you in my arms.

Do you know that I forgot to bring along my horse's rubbers and as a consequence he has exposed himself to cold several times from wet feet? I forgot also to bring along his toothbrush and his teeth are badly decayed. I shall have to get him a false set when I return to Lincoln. . . .

Mr. Barrows has kindly loaned me his stylus for this letter. He sends kind regards. As we are now 7,000 feet above the sea, I think more highly of him than ever.

Your affectionate husband,
George.[25]

Captain Yates's description of the Black Hills and the beauty it possessed was echoed in an article about the expedition in the August 11, 1874, edition of the *Detroit Free Press*. The article, written by a correspondent from the *St. Paul Tribune* traveling with the Seventh Cavalry, was well circulated at Fort Abraham Lincoln. Annie, Elizabeth, and a few other officers' wives speculated that the discoveries made during the trek through the region would further fuel the animosity between the Sioux, the army, and the settlers moving into the region.[26]

The country which the expedition has traversed has proved to be one of the most fertile and beautiful sections of the United States. Indications of gold were discovered about a week ago, and within two days, its presence in sufficient quantities abundantly to repay working has been established beyond a doubt. How large an area the gold section covers cannot be determined without further explorations, but the geological characteristics of the country, the research of our prospectors, and all the indications point to valuable fields. So far, we have obtained surface gold alone. Our miners hope yet to find a gold quartz lead. The expiration of the Sioux treaty will open to settlements a beautiful and highly productive area of country hitherto entirely unknown.[27]

Grass, water, and timber of several varieties are found in abundance and all of excellent qualities. Small fruits abound, game is plentiful, the valleys are well adapted for cattle-raising or agricultural purposes, while the scenery is lovely beyond description. It may be called a new Florida, and it may prove to be a new Eldorado. The command is in good health, and the explorations are being rapidly conducted.[28]

Captain Yates was home from the expedition in time for his daughter Bessie's birth. With little exception, life for the Yates family was pleasant and without incident until December 1874. What happened to cause disruption stemmed from an incident that had occurred in August 1873 when Lakota Sioux Chief Rain-in-the-Face led his warriors on a raid against members of the Seventh Cavalry. Among the military personnel killed during the attack were veterinary surgeon Dr. John Honsinger and a sutler named Augustus Baliran.[29] (A sutler was a person who followed the army and sold provisions to soldiers.)

Rain-in-the-Face and his men were driven from the confrontation by cavalry reinforcements. Word reached Custer just before Christmas in 1874 that the influential chief was residing at the Standing Rock Reservation in the Dakota Territory and boasting about killing the doctor and the sutler. Custer ordered Captain Yates, Lieutenant Tom Custer, and several companies within the Seventh to the reservation to arrest Rain-in-the-Face. The men returned to Fort Abraham Lincoln with the chief and placed him in the post jail. George explained to Custer that the apprehension of Rain-in-the-Face had created a great deal of unrest at the reservation and that the six thousand Indians who resided there were planning to leave. He also let Custer know the Indians were "splendidly armed."[30]

George and Annie discussed taking some time in the new year to travel east with their children, but General Custer refused leave for the captain. The relationship between the army and the Native Americans in the region was severely strained, and Custer didn't think it was wise to allow one of his most dependable officers to be away.[31]

The Yates family might have been bound to the post for a time, but their stay would not be boring. Many evenings during the long winter months from January to April 1875 were spent at the Custers' home with forty others in the general and Elizabeth's close circle. They enjoyed elaborate meals together, played games, and sang along with Maggie Calhoun as she played the piano the Custers had rented from St. Paul.[32]

In addition to the frivolity, the group engaged in lively discussions. The topic of conversation in April was the escape of Rain-in-the-Face from the post stockade. The chief returned to the reservation for a short time before going to the Powder River country and joining a war party there.[33]

When George and Annie were at their home alone, they talked about the third child they were expecting in the winter, and life beyond the army. Annie was struggling with her pregnancy in that time period and was frustrated with the lack of proper care from the young post

The officers' wives lived in these special quarters at Fort Lincoln, North Dakota.
COURTESY OF THE STATE HISTORICAL SOCIETY OF NORTH DAKOTA, B0686-00001

surgeon. He had little experience in the field of gynecology, and she was forced to rely on a laundress who was a part-time midwife for help.

Milnor Robert Yates was born on November 7, 1875. The proud parents began making plans to travel east the following summer so their children could meet both sets of grandparents. George applied for six months' leave starting in July 1876. Custer promised to approve his request.[34]

Annie's brothers, George and Richard Roberts, surprised her with a visit to Fort Abraham Lincoln in March 1876. She was thrilled to see them. Richard was a correspondent for the *New York Sun*, and had come to the post not only to see his sister, but also in hopes of accompanying Custer and the Seventh in the field to report on their work for the paper. He also volunteered to work as a teamster, handling the horses.[35]

The Roberts brothers were invited to take part in the gatherings at the Custers' home along with Annie and George and the usual collection of friends. After playing a game of charades, the officers, their wives, and the extended family members adjourned to the front porch of the quarters to have a group photograph taken. Once the pictures were taken, the party moved to a nearby shaded spot to enjoy ice cream and apple cider.

Annie, who had a reputation for being inquisitive, decided to ask Custer a few questions about his life before Fort Abraham Lincoln. Elizabeth later recounted the exchange in her journal.[36]

"She [Annie] asked him why he wore long hair and a velvet braided jacket and red necktie in the early days of the war. Autie responded with 'It began when I was little more than twenty-three. I commanded a brigade of three hundred men. I was but a boy just from West Point, and I was young and insignificant. Living with men in the brigade old enough to be my father, I wished them to know and acknowledge me at once from any part of the field. I chose a uniform that would catch their attention and individualize me.'"[37]

In the same journal entry, Elizabeth included a note Annie had written to her regarding Custer and her impressions of him.

The general's face was not that of a thoughtless, impulsive man. It was the somewhat warm but eager countenance of a man who had faced extraordinary responsibilities in his extreme youth. His eyes penetrating his broad, massive front [were those] of a thinker, not of one that would run into danger simply for the glory of it.[38]

He was a rapid reasoner and, in a few months, grasped a situation and acted upon it. His logic was instantaneous.

General Custer played chess at our get-togethers, as he did everything else. He seemed sometimes to be playing without thought, at random. Still, he was clever. He calculated every move and took as many concentrated moments as possible when a moment was important.[39]

Annie, George, and her brothers met with Custer and the other key members of the general and Elizabeth's close-knit group at the Custers' home in mid-May 1876. The subject everyone was talking about was the massacre of seven white settlers and two Indian women who resided with them at a camp along the Little Rock River in the southeastern portion of the Dakota Territory. According to the April 21, 1876, edition of the *St. Paul Tribune*, members of the Yankton Sioux tribe regularly visited the camp pretending to be friends with the people who lived there. "Finally, they came armed and at a signal fired and killed the entire party," the *Tribune* article read.[40]

Custer and his officers recognized that the report had upset the wives and assured them they would be safe at the post. In the unlikely event they found themselves under attack with no immediate protection or rescue on the horizon, the women were reminded of what they needed to do. "The protocol was drastic," Elizabeth later wrote, describing the actions army wives were to employ should they be taken captive. "Suicide was the mandate," she added. "We are to take our own lives before being captured. After the fact it's generally too late. Married women who have been taken are constantly looking for some way to commit suicide to escape the disgrace, and Indian braves will go to extremes to prevent that from happening."[41]

News that a number of Sioux warriors had been spotted on the Little Missouri River and were waiting for Custer and the Seventh Cavalry to leave the post was another serious subject discussed at the Custers' home in early May 1876. To determine the whereabouts of the "long-haired chief," the warriors had ventured dangerously close to Fort Abraham Lincoln. They had been sighted a few miles north of the fort, and Major Marcus Reno had dispatched scouts to investigate. Both Custer and George Yates acknowledged they were aware of the situation and would be dealing with the Sioux Indians on the Bighorn Expedition on which they were soon to embark.[42]

The setting and sober tone of the conversation at the Custers' quarters was reminiscent of a similar get-together at Fort Hays, Kansas, in early September 1870. The Custers, Annie, George, and the other friends of the general and Elizabeth's were spending a leisure moment picnicking under a cluster of maple trees. The evening before the outing, Annie had had a nightmare about the Seventh Cavalry, and Custer, in particular. Annie told Custer that in the dream she saw him shot in the head by an Indian.

Elizabeth recorded the exchange in her journal. "He [Custer] had cast himself on the ground under the blue sky while glancing over at me slowly swinging in a hammock. Suddenly he glanced up and explained to Annie, 'I'm the happiest man on the earth. I envy no one. With my wife and the Seventh Cavalry, the proudest command in the world, I would not change places with a king. Annie, I cannot die before my time comes and if by a bullet in the head—why not?"[43]

George and Annie's good-bye on May 17, 1876, was a tearful one. Not only was George leaving on another lengthy expedition, but Annie had shared with him the news she was expecting. Annie presented her husband with a watch to commemorate the occasion. It was a foggy and damp morning, and the inspirited strains of martial music from the Seventh Cavalry band floated through the air. One final kiss for his wife and children, and Captain Yates was off. He joined the line with Custer, two companies of cavalry, and forty scouts filing ahead of Charles Reynolds, chief scout, and F. F. Girard, interpreter, General A. H. Terry, and staff. Behind them were artillery, ambulances, and forage wagons, with infantry interspersed here and there, and in the rear and on the flanks of the column, a detachment of cavalry and infantry marching in two columns. Annie remarked to Elizabeth later that day that it was a "brilliant sight."[44]

From the time the Seventh Cavalry departed Fort Abraham Lincoln until mid-June, George Yates commanded a battalion of his own. His battalion was a part of three companies under Major Reno. George led his men along the Yellowstone River up the Powder River and back to the mouth of the Rosebud in search of Sioux Indians. He wrote a quick note to his brother-in-law, Richard, who was serving the Seventh as a civilian herder. After his horse gave out, Richard had to remain behind at the Powder River, seventy miles from the Little Bighorn. George wanted Richard to let Annie know where he was and what was going on. It was the last letter he would ever write.[45]

"General Custer and the remaining six companies met us on the march late yesterday afternoon," George wrote on June 21, 1876. "We are to start out at once with fifteen days more supplies to follow an Indian trail up [the] Rosebud with a very fair prospect of catching Indians. More than this I cannot say because I know nothing. . . . When we meet the steamer [*Far West*] again I know not. We do not know ourselves where the trail may lead. Circumstances must shape our course after today."[46]

Captain Yates's body was found just downhill from Custer's. One of his fingers had been cut off by the Native Americans involved in the battle, in order to acquire his ring. His gauntlets were missing, along with the watch Annie had given him the day he left.[47]

Annie took the news of her husband's death hard. The grief over the terrible loss took its toll on her physically, as well. Not long after George's death, she suffered a miscarriage. Both her brothers were with her to help her through the difficult time. George was now a memory, and, if not for her three children, the temptation to allow sorrow to overtake her would have proved too great. With her family's help, she determined not to dwell on the fact that George was no more but fought to remain thankful that he had been.[48]

A month after Captain Yates's funeral in Monroe and renting a home for herself and their children there, Annie decided it was time to find a job. The modest pension she received from the military was not enough to sustain them. Annie secured a position at Boyd's Young Ladies' Seminary in town, teaching French and music.[49]

Although Annie was busy teaching and raising her children, she still mourned the loss of her husband. Three months after the Battle of the Little Bighorn, newspapers continued to run stories about the incident, including horrific details of the condition of the soldiers who had died there. Some of the Sioux who joined in the fight had surrendered to authorities at the Standing Rock Reservation in the Dakota Territory, and others were captured at the Red Cloud Reservation in Wyoming Territory. Annie was not only reminded her husband was gone when she looked into the faces of her sons and daughter, but also whenever she read the paper. Only the other widows who lost their husbands at the Last Stand could understand the relentless sorrow.[50]

By the late fall of 1876, the number of condolence letters the Widow Yates received had slowed significantly. One of the last heartbreaking notes arrived in November from her brother-in-law, Francis D. Yates. Francis operated a trading store at the Red Cloud Reservation. Enclosed with the short message expressing his sadness over her husband's death, Francis sent along an item that belonged to Annie. It was the watch she had given George the last time they had seen one another. A Native American had brought the watch into Francis's store and tried to make a trade for it. Francis recognized the item as Annie's and confiscated the timepiece.[51]

The grief the widows of the officers slain at the Battle of the Little Bighorn felt was compounded by the fact that they had no formal graves of their loved ones to visit. Custer and his troops were buried where they fell on June 27, 1876. Surviving officers and soldiers of the Seventh Cavalry placed their fallen comrades in shallow graves. The ground was hard, and they only had a handful of shovels to do the job, so most of the dead were covered with a limited amount of dirt or brush. Markers had been placed where the officers lay. The name of each man had been written on a piece of paper, the paper slid into a spent cartridge shell, and then the shell hammered into the wooden marker.[52]

Annie, Elizabeth, and Nettie Smith, along with the four other officers' widows and family members, began petitioning the army to exhume the dead and transport them home in early September 1876.[53]

Like the other widows, Annie wanted her husband's body returned to her so he could receive a proper burial at a location where she and her children could pay their respects. Annie felt that only then could she get on with the business of living.

Chapter Three

Hidden Away

Newspapers often referred to Maggie Custer Calhoun as the "most sorrowful" of all the Little Bighorn widows. She not only had to cope with the death of her husband, James Calhoun, but also the deaths of three brothers and a nephew. She did not handle the catastrophic loss as gracefully or as quickly as the other widows. The tragedy engulfed her mind, body, and soul. For weeks she refused to leave her parents' home. Her heart was shattered. Memories of her beloved spouse mixed with the recollections of Custer, Thomas, Boston, and Harry regularly ambushed her, making it nearly impossible for her to move forward.[1]

Often too grief-stricken to leave her room, meals were brought to her, but they seemed more a source of sadness than nourishment. The dishes—like chicken with dressing, biscuits, taffy kisses, and fried potatoes—reminded her of those she had prepared to bring to Custer and Elizabeth's home at Fort Abraham Lincoln, for their weekly soirees. Custer's clan spent many long winter hours together sharing meals, playing charades, and discussing frontier life. Maggie recalled how much James had enjoyed her culinary contributions. He often bragged about her cooking, and listed her "gifting" in the kitchen as being one of her many talents he most appreciated. He also liked to hear her play the piano. Several of the officers' wives with the Seventh Cavalry could play, but Maggie was an accomplished pianist, having been trained at Boyd's Seminary in Monroe. Requests for her to entertain had been made at every gathering.[2]

James Calhoun, born on August 24, 1845, in Cincinnati, Ohio, met Maggie Custer at Fort Leavenworth, Kansas, in the summer of 1870.

He fought for the Union during the Civil War and continued his service in the army after the conflict ended. As a second lieutenant with the Thirty-Second Infantry, he was stationed at Camp Warner in Oregon in 1867. He was transferred to Camp Grant in Arizona where he was promoted to first lieutenant. His work took him to a variety of army posts in the West, and he participated in a number of skirmishes with Native Americans who were opposed to the military's presence.

In May 1870, James, then with the Twenty-First Infantry, reported for duty at Fort Leavenworth and there made the acquaintance of General George Armstrong Custer's sister. Maggie had to travel to the post from Monroe to visit her brother and sister-in-law. The two were enam-

From left to right: Margaret Custer Calhoun; George Custer's younger brother, Boston Custer; Captain Thomas Ward Custer; and General Custer's nephew, Harry Armstrong (Autie) Reed
COURTESY OF THE MONROE COUNTY MUSEUM SYSTEM, MONROE, MICHIGAN, AND THE STATE HISTORICAL SOCIETY OF NORTH DAKOTA, C1627-00001 (CAPTAIN THOMAS WARD CUSTER)

ored with one another from the beginning, and Elizabeth encouraged Custer to invite the officer to spend time with family and friends on a hunting expedition on the plains around Fort Hays, Kansas. James eagerly accepted.[3]

From mid-June to August of 1870, Maggie and James were inseparable. By the end of the expedition the couple had fallen in love and were petitioning Custer to have James transferred to the Seventh Cavalry. Custer agreed, made the appropriate requests, and placed his future brother-in-law in command of L Company. James wrote Custer a letter dated April 23, 1871, to express his gratitude for orchestrating the desired

Lieutenant James Calhoun
COURTESY OF THE DENVER PUBLIC
LIBRARY, SPECIAL COLLECTIONS

transfer. "My dear General," he began, "I have just received my commission as 1st Lieutenant in the 7th Cavalry, and it reminds me more vividly than ever how many, many times I am under obligation to you for your very great kindness to me in my troubles. I shall do my best to prove my gratitude. If the time comes you will not find me wanting. . . . Lt. James Calhoun."[4]

Maggie and James were married on March 12, 1872, at the Methodist church in Monroe, Michigan. He was twenty-six, and she was twenty. The Custer family and friends sat on the left and the Calhoun family on the right. James's father, James Sr., had died in 1864, but his mother Charlotte, his two sisters, Lottie and Mary, and his brother, Frederic, were present. Frederic, serving as best man, met his future wife at the wedding. Maggie's niece, Emma Reed, was smitten with him, and the two agreed to correspond after the ceremony. They married seven years later, on February 24, 1879. Maggie's brother, Tom, signed the Monroe County Marriage Record as the witness to the union.[5]

Shortly after the Calhouns' wedding, the newlyweds traveled to the military post at Elizabethtown, Kentucky, where James was assigned.

Custer Family Home in Monroe, Michigan
COURTESY OF THE STATE HISTORICAL SOCIETY OF NORTH DAKOTA, A5672-00001

Custer, commander of the post, and Elizabeth were there to welcome the couple when they arrived. Maggie had always admired Elizabeth for accompanying Custer in the field, and she wanted to do the same with her husband. Although she found Kentucky less than congenial, she was grateful she could be with James.

Letters from Elizabeth to Maggie written in the fall of 1871 painted a somber picture of the outpost and contributed to her bleak opinion of the location before she arrived.[6]

Imagine yourself your grandmother to get an idea of this place. Everything is old, particularly the women. The old madam landlady [the Custers were staying at the Hills' boardinghouse in Elizabethtown until they found a home] entered into conversation with me at the first meal. I, smiling, trying to keep up with what I hoped were well-studied remarks, when mistakenly I said, "I don't think many ladies have fine suits of hair." The old false front I was addressing nearly dropped off.

The old standing corner clock has not been allowed to run down for forty-five years. The dog is sweet sixteen and can scarcely walk. An old gentleman boarder from the old school is equally unsteady on his legs. But tho [sic] over seventy, [he] wishes to marry again. . . . No, not the landlady who was his old sweetheart, but a young girl.

To keep flies off the table an infernal flying machine runs its length, pieces of board about three feet square, attached in a series to a rope with a red rag hanging from it. This [is pulled] in order to agitate the boards, so that we dine to music.

The most active inhabitant of the place is a pig.[7]

Despite the dismal setting, the Custers, their family, and their close friends found ways to make their temporary home inviting. Custer and Elizabeth hosted hunting trips and dinners for the officers of the Seventh Cavalry and their wives. Maggie contributed to the festivities by providing specially prepared desserts and helping to organize parlor games to be played after the meal.

The Calhouns were a well-respected couple within the Custer clan. James was referred to as "the Adonis of the Seventh" because of his good looks. Maggie was always pleasant and happy to help wherever she was needed.[8] Annie Gibson, wife of Lieutenant Francis M. Gibson with the Seventh Cavalry, described Maggie in glowing terms in her memoirs. "Maggie Calhoun was a lot of fun," she wrote, "and had the qualities of her brothers which made friends readily."[9]

Maggie's health suffered while at Elizabethtown. She was plagued with headaches accompanied with either chills or a fever. The proprietor of the hotel, where she and James lived with several other married officers, took pity on her during those days when she was feeling ill. The woman would prepare a mixture of wishbone flower blossoms with catnip tea for her.[10]

The Calhouns' time in Kentucky was brief. By February 1873, the Seventh Cavalry was bound for Memphis, Tennessee, and then on to the Dakota Territory. Maggie, as well as the other officers' wives, would make the journey to the next post by steamship and by train. They boarded the steamer in Louisville and traveled on the Ohio River to Cairo,

Illinois. The Illinois Central Railroad transported the women to Yankton, Dakota, where a massive snowstorm awaited them.[11]

Newspapers throughout the country reported on the movement of the troops and their families into the Dakota Territory. "On the morning of April 13th, the Seventh Cavalry, under Custer, had arrived and were arranging their camp," the May 3, 1873, edition of the *Raleigh News* noted. "Canvas tents were being pitched, the horses were picketed in rows, the laundresses and children were scolding shrilly and tumbling about gleefully in the scenes new to them. A mild wind was blowing from the west and southwest and a light rain falling. On the plains, the tender green of the new grass could be seen here and there, a sparse embroidery on the browner and duskier herbage of last year, and flocks of summer birds flew and twittered intermittently. It was spring, rather wet and indubitably bleak, but spring, nevertheless.[12]

"Then a storm came in suddenly as a great hurricane. The sky grew pale, then darkened to an ominous yellowish gray. The rain grew colder, then turned to sleet, then to snow, which fell lightly till noon. Then the wind strengthened. Soon, the air became black with snow."[13]

Maggie and Elizabeth decided to remain with their husbands at this juncture, but the other officers' wives continued on, taking a riverboat up the Mississippi on a thirty-four-day venture that would eventually bring them to Fort Rice. Maggie and James found a place to stay in Yankton until the Seventh was ready to make the more than four-hundred-mile march from the southern part of the Dakotas to the northern. Both Maggie and Elizabeth rode with their spouses in front of two long columns of soldiers.[14]

When the Calhouns arrived at Fort Rice in early June 1873, they were sorely disappointed. Established in 1864, the small military installation consisted of a few buildings made from cottonwood logs. There were four rustic company barracks with kitchens, seven officers' quarters in need of repair, storehouses, and what was once a post hospital. The condition of the entire post was unsuitable for women.[15]

Maggie and Elizabeth contemplated looking beyond the crude accommodations and considered living in tents if they could be found. They were waiting until their belongings arrived before they decided how to proceed. When the steamer delivered their personal possessions and household items several days after they reached the fort, the women found most of their things were ruined. Books, pictures, bedding, and dresses were all destroyed.[16]

"Our household effects and trunks were delivered to us in very sorry condition," Elizabeth wrote in her book, *Boots and Saddles*. "They had been carelessly stored on the wharf without any covering, during all the storms that drenched us coming up river. . . ."[17]

"Our sister's husband [James] helped her unpack her clothes and his soaked uniforms. He was dignified and reserved by nature, but on that occasion the barriers were broken. I heard him ask Margaret to excuse him while he went outside the tent to make some remarks to himself that he felt the occasion demanded."[18]

At the urging of her husband, Maggie agreed to return to her family's home in Monroe via train. Elizabeth did the same. The Seventh Cavalry was scheduled to accompany a survey team of more than a thousand men whose job it was to find a route for the Northern Pacific Railroad. Wives were not authorized to follow their husbands on the trek.[19]

It was estimated that Custer and his troops would be in the field for more than sixty days. Maggie and James would have to rely on letters to get them through until they saw one another again. Maggie didn't relish the thought of being so far away from her husband. She was safe at her parents' house but worried he would meet some harm at the hand of the Native Americans who made the area their home.

James's letters to his wife revealed the basics of his everyday life but nothing of his gambling habit. Custer and his officers routinely engaged in games of poker in the evenings.[20] According to letters Custer wrote Elizabeth, James was a poor card player and lost most nights. "The officers have been sitting night and day, playing poker," Custer explained to Elizabeth in a letter dated June 26, 1873. "They are now in Dr. H's tent, next to mine. I carry Tom's [Custer] funds now. Mr. C. [Calhoun] began playing as soon as we left Rice, and only stopped night before last, from lack of funds. He borrowed $20 from me, but cannot get anymore from me, nor any from Tom, since Tom has to borrow to play. I hope C. will lose every time he sits down. Otherwise, he will return to winter quarters with nothing to go on with."[21]

Elizabeth was troubled by the news Custer had shared with her. She didn't want James's out-of-control gambling to lead to out-of-control drinking. She felt it was her duty to share the situation with Maggie in hopes she could help her husband fight the compulsion.

The longer Maggie was apart from James the more depressed she became. Depression often turned to worry after reading newspaper accounts of the Yellowstone Expedition. An article in the August 27, 1873, edition of the *Bismarck Tribune* left Maggie imagining she'd never see James again. Earlier in the month, the Sioux had tried to ambush Custer and his troops. More than three hundred Native Americans were involved in the failed attempt to overtake the soldiers. In the process of driving the Sioux back, two unarmed civilians were killed, as well as a private with the Seventh Cavalry. The soldiers pursued the Native Americans to the banks of the Yellowstone River, where they noticed the number of Sioux had increased to more than five hundred.[22]

"Custer and Adjutant Ketchum had their horses killed under them," the *Bismarck Tribune* article read. "Chas. Beaton, Seventh Cavalry, had his thigh broken by a bullet. The Sioux were dressed in [Indian] Agency clothing and threw away Winchester rifles and ammunition, showing that they were recently supplied."[23]

Maggie's worry would not be relieved until she was reunited with James in November 1873. Maggie and the other wives of the Seventh Cavalry soldiers were to meet their spouses at Fort Abraham Lincoln in the northern portion of the Dakota Territory. Built in 1872, the fort was populated with troops whose job it was to protect the construction of the Northern Pacific Railroad. The young post possessed new quarters for the troops and the officers and their families. Compared to the rustic settings of Fort Rice and Elizabethtown, Fort Lincoln was Shangri-la. The pristine condition of the post, however, could not eclipse the concerns that came with living there. The remote facility was surrounded by Native Americans who resented the presence of the white man and who were not afraid to challenge them.[24]

Snowy and icy weather frequently overwhelmed the region, making it next to impossible to venture outside. Maggie was willing to withstand anything as long as she could be with James. According to Maggie, the two and half years the couple spent at Fort Abraham Lincoln were the happiest of their lives.[25]

The Custers' elegant, two-story home, complete with insulated walls and numerous fireplaces, was a spot of civilization as "Eastern" as Custer and Elizabeth could make it in the midst of the isolated Dakotas. They had a piano in the parlor and a billiard table in the den. The Calhouns were frequent guests of Custer and his wife, along with the other officers in his command and their wives. During the summer months, the forty members of the group would go on hunting trips, and, in the winter, they spent time together at banquets and post dances.[26]

Group photograph of Elizabeth and George Custer with a few of their friends on the porch of their quarters at Fort Lincoln; Lieutenant James Calhoun is seated in the middle of the top row; Margaret Calhoun is seated to the right of him.
COURTESY OF THE NATIONAL PARK SERVICE, LITTLE BIGHORN BATTLEFIELD NATIONAL MONUMENT

When James and the other soldiers were ordered elsewhere, as in the Black Hills Expedition of 1874, Maggie concentrated on her sewing and correspondence with family and friends back in Monroe. Nothing out of the ordinary occurred in the Calhouns' lives. They were a typical army couple with plans for a family and a home of their own beyond the military years. Neither could have foreseen the heartbreak to come.[27]

An article in the May 4, 1876, edition of the *Boston Globe* reported on the expedition that would separate Maggie and James forever. In January 1876, the commissioner of Indian Affairs sent a message to Sitting Bull, a Hunkpapa Sioux chief who organized tribes refusing to give up their ancestral homes to fight against the white settlers who demanded they return to the reservation. "Sitting Bull having failed to take any notice of this request, his case was turned over to General Sherman, and the consequence is the expedition starting from Fort Lincoln," the *Boston Globe* article read. "The expedition is composed of the Seventh Cavalry principally, with another infantry to guard the train, and will be under the immediate command of General Terry. The object is to find Sitting Bull and his gang and administer to them such punishment as will compel them to return to their reservation."[28]

Sitting Bull and the other Native Americans could not be compelled.

More than ten months after the death of her husband, Maggie Calhoun continued to grapple with debilitating grief. Maggie's niece Emma and friend Annie Yates were great comforts, but she missed Elizabeth. Her sister-in-law, upon whom she relied the most for strength and encouragement, had decided to move to New York to find work and to help her get beyond the tragedy. Maggie and Elizabeth wrote one another often, but without the same comforting effect.

When George and Custer died, it was expected that the widows would return to Monroe to care for the Custer brothers' mother and father. The thought of having to fulfill that obligation alone, particularly when her strength and will were shaky, added to Maggie's distress. She was hesitant to share with Elizabeth the toll her leaving had had on her, but others refused to keep quiet.[29]

Maggie wrote on May 12, 1877, in response to a letter from Elizabeth expressing concern for Maggie's health:

My dearest Libbie,

First of all I may as well own up and tell you all about myself in as few words as possible. Annie said she wrote you I was poorly. I had not been feeling well for a number of days but Sunday one of my awful headaches came on. Lay down much of the day and evening on Monday. Suffered all Monday night and not able to be up on Tuesday and have kept to my bed ever since with the exception of a few vain attempts at sitting up.[30]

My head aches much of the time, but the greatest trouble has been several sinking spells, not actual faints, but my strength was all taken out of me. I was very sick night before last—nearly all night—but with whiskey and Lily's rubbing I came through, though was in a very dilapidated condition all day yesterday. Did not have the doctor until yesterday morning. He said I had done very wrong to allow myself to run down so without sending for him. I am much better today as this letter testifies. I feel like a selfish idiot telling you all these particulars, but please don't scold . . .

Your letters are regular feasts for me. I want to see you so badly and love you so dearly that it is with great effort that I resist the temptation to be spooney. But now I must stop. I'll get well soon and eat oatmeal but am afraid it will make me too fat. . . .

Will write when ever [sic] I can.

Your devoted sister,

Maggie[31]

Maggie's situation hadn't improved three days later when she again wrote Elizabeth on May 15, 1877.

"I must write you tho' [*sic*] I know every line hurts me. I sat up this a.m. for fifteen minutes and hope to repeat and increase the dose this p.m., fever, headache, and strength permitting. I see very few people and talk and am talked to very little, but I feel myself that I would be better not to speak or be spoken to for days. Dear knows it is lonely and forlorn enough as it is—shut up in this dark room with an occasional word.[32]

"Do not worry about me, dear Libbie. I expect to be well in a few days now. Mother is not quite so well today. Write whenever you can. Don't work too steadily. Your devoted sister, Maggie."[33]

It was not uncommon for well-known people to travel to Monroe to visit the Custer family and pay their respects. In early June 1877, Miss G. A. Davis, an artist with *Frank Leslie's Illustrated Newspaper*, came to see the Custer family and express her sympathy. Maggie's letter to Elizabeth dated June 5, 1877, focused on the thoughtful guest.[34]

Where shall I commence? Well, I never was so full of talk in all my life—seems to me—as since I find myself limited by your absence, my dear sister. I feel exhausted before I begin my letter at the thought that it must leave so much unsaid. I am too deep in unanswered letters, for me, as my illness has prevented me keeping up my correspondence, except with you and I just have to write to you. But to the point.

First, I will tell you as briefly as possible of the visit I have had from Miss Georgia Davis. She has been in California for Frank Leslie's party. They passed thru [sic] here yesterday on their way to Detroit. They stopped over to see you and [she] was disappointed when she found you were not here. I entertained her as best I could, and she really seemed to enjoy her visit. Annie [Yates] came down while she was here. She [Georgia] expected her party back last night, but they did not come, so she stayed with us till this morning. Father and I accompanied her to the depot. I like her very much and enjoyed her visit exceedingly, though I was not feeling very well. . . .

And now my darling sister, I will try to say something regarding the news contained in your last letter. [Elizabeth had taken a job at the New York Sanitary Commission.] No, I'll not try, I'll be frank and let selfishness as well as everything else have a little expression. My heart sank within me when I read that the separation which I had looked forward to as a possibility in the dim future, had really come so soon. I can't tell you how I feel about it, my dear sister, only that life seemed much more unendurable than it did before your letter came. I know I am selfish. I can't help it, and yet my selfishness is not so great that I would sacrifice your desires to my wishes, but I grieve for myself, that is all.

Yesterday, because of Miss Davis's presence, I had to exercise self-control, tho' [sic] she may have seen the tears which would force themselves into my eyes, but I knew the outburst must come, and all alone in my room today I had to give up for a little while; I appreciate thoroughly your desire and motive in this matter, and have no word or thought of censure for you, but my dear sister, I am so afraid you have undertaken too much. You will overwork yourself. One of the enterprizes [sic] seems to me would have been as much as you should undertake. I am afraid you will injure your health. . . .

I can't bear to think of you enduring so much. I know you will do too much, and would Autie like that? Please take care of yourself, for this reason if no other, that your strength, if judiciously used, may enable you to minister to others all your life, whereas, if you over do [sic], you may incapacitate yourself for further usefulness.

I told Father this morning that you would not be home before September and why you would not. He received the announcement with no reply except an intensified expression of countenance resembling the one which characterized his face when he informed us that Hays was really elected. . . .

And now I have had my say in regard to your new field and for the future I shall cultivate unselfishness; will try not to complain. Yes, I think I can safely say that I will not complain but with God's help will try to endure without you the burden which I felt your presence must help me to bear. . . .

Annie's eyes filled with tears when I told her what you had written me about not coming back. I do not believe you have any idea how much you are missed. Though I would not keep you in Monroe, if I could, still I can not [sic] help missing you and needing you all the time. Dear Libbie, I feel sure that you have no idea of how much you are to me. . . .

Yours devotedly,
Maggie[35]

As the first anniversary of the Battle of the Little Bighorn grew near, Maggie's spirits fell. Although she seldom left her parents' home, she was aware of what was happening in town and out west through the newspapers that came her way. Reports from the Dakota Territory about the skirmishes between the army and the Native Americans upset her. A story in the May 28, 1877, edition of the *Bismarck Tribune* made her weep. The Twenty-Second Cavalry and the Fifth Infantry "attacked an Indian village on Little Muddy Creek, a branch of the Rosebud, ninety miles from the mouth of the Tongue River." Among the items seized from the village were 450 ponies and horses. Also confiscated were 54 lodges and their entire contents, consisting of an abundance of all kinds of provisions from the Indian Agency, many saddles, guns, officers' clothing, and other articles taken from the Seventh Cavalry in the Custer fight.

Maggie hoped some of the items found once belonged to James.[36]

For months Elizabeth, Annie, and the other officers' widows had been pressing General Phil Sheridan, head of the Department of the Missouri, to exhume their husbands' bodies so they could be moved and given a proper burial. The army was in the process of transporting the remains from the battlefield to Fort Abraham Lincoln. Soon James would be leaving Montana, bound for Kansas, where he was to be laid to rest. Memories of him and their life together drove Maggie to tears again and once more placed her health in jeopardy.[37]

"Dearest Sister, I am not feeling particularly well and for once in my life my appearance does not belie my words," Maggie wrote Elizabeth on June 18, 1877. "I really look quite pale and uninteresting—it will not be long, I presume, before it can be said, 'red as a rose is she.'"[38]

Maggie's unhappiness spilled over again in the next letter she wrote Elizabeth, on June 24, 1877. "O! these sad, sad anniversaries. How I miss you and wish for your presence on these days especially—helping me as you have in days gone by—by your tenderness and sympathy—though unspoken to bear my heavy burden."[39]

Maggie's relapse made it questionable if she would be able to attend James's funeral, scheduled for August 4, 1877. Elizabeth was fearful of the emotional effect missing the service would have on Maggie, but she didn't want Maggie's health to get worse, either.

A letter from Maggie to Elizabeth written on July 24, 1877, set her worries to rest.[40]

> *I have decided to go to Leavenworth. You will think me changeable and perhaps self-willed and imprudent, but listen while I explain, and I think you will understand and not wholly disapprove of my decision.[41]*
>
> *For the last ten days I have been so much better than for weeks previous. My appetite is really wonderful. Three times a day I eat heartily and am stronger and better [in] every way and I feel that I am equal to the trip to Leavenworth. Being as well as I am, I feel that there is no reason why I should not go and that I should all my life regret and reproach myself should I remain away.*
>
> *It seems too hard to think of their precious remains being laid away and not one of us there. So, please, dear sister, do not blame me and do not feel anxious about me. I shall be careful. Shall pray much for strength and do all I can to save what I have. I feel that the going there will be a comfort to me all my life, and I feel so sure that I am right in deciding to go now that I am so much better. Blame no one but myself for this decision, dear sister, for everybody has opposed it, but I came up with the intention of going if my health justified.[42]*

James Calhoun's remains, as well as Thomas Custer's, George Yates's, Donald McIntosh's, and Algernon Smith's, arrived at Fort Leavenworth, Kansas, on Tuesday, July 31, 1877. The officers' coffins were placed on a platform at the fort chapel, and members of the honor guard kept a vigilant watch over the slain soldiers until the funeral.

Maggie traveled from Michigan with Annie Yates and her children. Her health did not falter during the days leading to the memorial service. Maggie wrote Elizabeth that she made it to her destination without incident and in surprisingly good physical condition.[43]

"Dearest Libbie, only a few lines to tell you of my safe arrival here," Maggie noted to her sister-in-law on July 29, 1877. "Reached here last night after a very comfortable journey. Stayed in Grand Rapids until 11 o'clock yesterday a.m. arriving at 7 p.m.... I am feeling really very well. Was but little fatigued, so please, dear sister, do not worry about me.... How I wish you were here with us. Hastily but lovingly yours, Maggie."[44]

James Calhoun's brother Frederic was by Maggie's side at the church service. The five coffins in front of the altar were draped in the folds of the Stars and Stripes. After the memorial, the coffins were placed on five artillery caissons and moved to the cemetery. A military procession followed the caissons, each drawn by two bay horses. Seventh Cavalry officers walked on either side of the vehicles. Mourners followed behind the caissons. Frederic supported Maggie, who at times believed she wouldn't make it through the solemn event.[45]

During the march to the cemetery, minute guns* were fired, flags lowered to half-mast, and all work on the post suspended. After the religious ceremonies at the graves, a salute was fired by the troops over the coffins as they were lowered into the ground. Maggie dropped flowers into James's grave, and the wives and families of the other men did likewise.[46]

Maggie was back in Michigan by mid-August. The funeral had brought a wave of memories that washed over her, and she fought the temptation to again hide herself away in her parents' home to mourn James's death. Letters from Elizabeth helped her realize how much she wanted to move beyond her grief, as her sister-in-law had done. Elizabeth had found a way to be true to her husband's memory and to carry on in the process. If not for the obligation she felt she had to her parents, Maggie might have been persuaded to leave Monroe and hurry to Elizabeth in New York. However, Maria Custer struggled with poor health, and Emanuel had been called to Clarksburg, Virginia, to say good-bye to his own dying mother. For the time, Maggie would have to live vicariously through Elizabeth.[47]

Maggie wrote the following to Elizabeth, on August 15, 1877:

Dearest Sister,

Every time I have written you during the past month I have forgotten to tell you the following interesting items about yourself.

---

* Minute guns are discharged once every minute (usually as part of a military funeral).

After you wrote me about your occupation and said I could make it public, I took particular pains to tell just what you were doing. That you were secretary etc. and on a committee for visiting one or two wards in Bellevue Hospital and gave full explanations. Results, just before I went to Petoskey [a city in Michigan] I heard that you had sole charge of two hospitals in New York City and that you were living there under an assumed name. Then I received a letter from Lottie [Maggie's sister-in-law] in which she said Mrs. Tickesor had come to her and asked her if she knew that Mrs. Custer was in Europe taking care of the wounded soldiers from the Eastern war. Of course, Lottie was only amused and wondered how such stories could originate. But to think Monroe people, after all my pains, knowing their propensity, should get things so twisted.⁴⁸

Libbie, I have $35.00. The result of Bubbie's [her pet name for James] letters last summer to World *and* Graphic *[an illustrated weekly paper], and I have wanted to invest in something special that I could always keep. I think dear Bubbie would be so pleased to have me do this, but I have been unable all these months to think of anything until the other day. I happened to think of a necklace and locket Mrs. Edgerly had of onyx. Now such a necklace and locket may cost a thousand for all I know, or it may cost $25.00 or $30.00. I write to you to ask you when you have time to price something of [the] kind and let me know.*

I saw a young lady in deep mourning this summer who wore onyx, and as I cannot wear the pretty gold necklace Bubbie gave me, I know he would be pleased if I could have an onyx one. Especially if I prized his literary receipts (about which we often joked) enough to invest it in a remembrance. Remember, I shall not be disappointed if the necklace and locket are far beyond my means, as I know nothing of the value of onyx and only ask for information. . . .

O! I want to see you so badly. Goodbye for this time.

Ever your devoted sister, Maggie.

I have a good appetite (almost too good to be lady-like) and am quite well. Pluck does do lots.⁴⁹

Maggie did try not to be at the mercy of the whims of grief, but, more than a year after James's death, she continued to struggle to keep from being consumed with sadness. "I did not write any letters yesterday," she confessed to Elizabeth on September 3, 1877. "I could not. I was not sick physically, but my poor heart and mind were that state which needs not to be described to you to be understood."[50]

CHAPTER FOUR

The Widowed Moment

MOLLY GARRETT MCINTOSH declined to attend the burial of her husband, First Lieutenant Donald McIntosh, at Fort Leavenworth on August 3, 1877. She left Fort Abraham Lincoln in the Dakota Territory in late July 1876, a broken woman with no idea how she would go on without her beloved.

First Lieutenant McIntosh, the thirty-seven-year-old commander of the Seventh Cavalry's Company G, fell with the other officers at the Battle of the Little Bighorn. His remains had been identified by his brother-in-law, Lieutenant Frank Gibson. Gibson was with the Seventh's Company H and part of the detail dispatched to the scene to recover and bury the bod-

Molly Garrett McIntosh
FROM THE COLLECTION OF TIM TYTLE

ies of his fellow soldiers. According to a report from Lieutenant Charles F. Roe, who rode with Gibson on the detail, Donald's body was found close to the banks of the Little Bighorn River. He had been stripped and scalped, his head "pounded to jelly." His remains were identified by the special sleeve buttons found near where his body lay. The "gutta-percha" buttons (made of decorative, molded latex) had been a present from Molly, given to him just before he had ridden out with General Custer to Montana. She secretly had had them sewn on his uniform.[1]

Not long after leaving Fort Abraham Lincoln to return to Baltimore to live with her mother, Molly learned of the condition of her husband's body. She was desperate to find out what had happened to Donald. She knew he had kept a journal of his activities, a small, dark book he'd always kept tucked in the pocket of his uniform. Molly wanted to know if the journal had been located. She also wanted to know if his wedding ring had been taken by the Indians after the battle. The ring, gold with a small diamond, bore the initials inside of both Donald and Molly, along with the number sixty-six, for 1866, the year the two were married. Neither his journal nor his wedding ring was located. Molly's sister Katherine, wife of Lieutenant Frank Gibson, thought it was cruel not to let her know the truth and gently explained what Frank had shared with her about Donald's death. Molly was grateful, but imagining how her husband had suffered drove her to her parents' home, where she shut herself away.[2]

Molly's father, Milton Garrett, had passed away in 1869, and her mother Mary was alone and in poor health. Molly was there to take care of her. Apart from Mary, Molly saw no one. She isolated herself from the world to grieve the loss of her spouse alone.[3]

Like the other widows, Molly reflected on the last time she had seen her husband. It was the morning of May 17, 1876, and Donald was marching in step around the parade field with the other members of the Seventh Cavalry at Fort Abraham Lincoln. The band that rode behind them was playing "Garryowen." Donald and the other married officers had bid their wives good-bye a few yards outside the post. Molly and her first lieutenant embraced and promised to write as often as possible. Having lived the life of a cavalry soldier's wife for ten years, she was no stranger to tearful farewells. According to Katherine, Molly believed living on the edge with her husband in the field was a "hazard of existence that tempted adventurous souls and lured them west."[4]

When Molly and Donald had married on October 30, 1866, she was blissfully unaware of the difficulties that lay ahead for an army wife. Her father Milton anticipated she would endure severe hardship and refused to give the union his blessing. He was convinced that "the plains were no fit setting for any man's daughter." Her mother didn't disapprove of Donald but worried the unstable life of a military dependent would be too much strain for Molly.[5]

Donald had met his future wife in 1865 while serving as the chief clerk for Assistant Quartermaster and Brigadier General Daniel Rucker in Washington, DC. Molly was a well-mannered lady whose parents wanted for her a man of means and position. Donald McIntosh was an educated man from Alberta, Canada. His Scottish father and grandfather had been fur trappers for the Hudson Bay Company. His mother was a descendant of Red Jacket, a member of the Seneca tribe and chief of the Six Nations.[6]

One of the first army posts to which the newlyweds were ordered to report was Fort Harker, Kansas. The war between the United States and the Native Americans on the Great Plains had prompted military officials to fortify the outpost with soldiers. Those soldiers were to escort wagon train parties across the prairie to points west. The young couple remained at Fort Harker until the spring of 1869. At that time, Donald was appointed a first lieutenant with the Seventh Cavalry and transferred to Fort Larned. It was there the two met George and Elizabeth Custer. By the summer of that same year, the McIntoshes were welcomed members of Custer's coterie.[7]

"Tosh," as he was affectionately called by Custer and the other members of the Seventh Cavalry, experienced his fair share of trouble coming up through the ranks. Molly was beside him every step of the way. In May 1868, he was assigned to serve as an escort to a railroad survey party at the Plum Creek station in Nebraska. The previous month, Native Americans in the area had killed four railroad employees. Donald and the other soldiers he would ride with were to protect members of the Union Pacific Railroad. Shortly after McIntosh arrived at Plum Creek, he became sick with dysentery. He was ordered to return to Fort Harker where Molly spent the next ten months nursing him back to health.[8]

General Custer proved his fondness for the McIntoshes by helping the pair through another difficult time in 1870. Colonel Samuel D. Sturgis, commander of the Seventh Cavalry, didn't care for First Lieutenant

McIntosh and had petitioned for his dismissal from the army. In the report the colonel submitted to his superior officers in Washington, DC, he noted that McIntosh was "eminently inefficient." He had shown "extreme indifference to his official duties, giving him the appearance of desiring to render the smallest possible service compatible with absolute security of his commission. If he were an enlisted man, he would pass as a malingerer."[9]

When Donald was eventually brought before the Board of Review in Washington, Custer was standing with him, testifying to his good character. The charges against him were ultimately dropped.[10]

In addition to the McIntoshes joining the Custers and their clan on an outing at Big Creek Camp outside Fort Hays, Kansas, in the summer of 1869, Molly and Donald accompanied the group on a buffalo hunt in the summer of 1870. Molly's sister Katherine was also a part of the getaway. Katherine had been suffering with a persistent cough, and Molly believed the change in environment and temperature would help stifle the affliction. In her autobiography, Katherine described her sister as "physically strong and fearless." She described Donald as a man with a "keen sense of humor" who had a "quiet voice and manner." Katherine also noted he was one of the most beloved officers of the regiment. "He combined the brilliant mind of a student with a marked flair for military science."[11]

Katherine admired Molly and Donald's marriage. They were devoted to one another and embraced every moment they had together. Molly was always eager to celebrate Donald's accomplishments. Katherine recalled a wine party her sister held in her husband's honor on August 23, 1870, to commemorate a raise in rank. Fellow Seventh Cavalry soldier Lieutenant William W. Cooke contributed a story about the soiree that appeared in the September 1, 1870, edition of the *Leavenworth Weekly Times*.[12] "The monotony of camp life was broken a little last evening by the uncorking of bottles in acknowledgement of the promotion of Lt. Daniel [*sic*] McIntosh of the Seventh Cavalry to First Lieutenant," the article read. "May his well-deserved promotion rest lightly upon him as he joins the grade of that 'long suffering and well deserving class' of First Lieutenants."[13]

Katherine returned to her family's home on the East Coast in late summer of 1870 feeling better than she had in months, and without the nagging cough. The time she had spent with her sister and brother-in-law was exciting, and she witnessed how much in love Donald and Molly were every day she was with them. Katherine left their company hoping to visit again and convinced she wanted the same life the McIntoshes had.[14]

From the Great Plains, Molly and Donald traveled to the Colorado Territory to report to company commanders at Fort Lyons on February 11, 1871. Three months later, the couple was transferred to South Carolina. Various companies were sent to the South to help deal with the civil unrest there. The Ku Klux Klan was committing acts of violence against Black Americans, and order needed to be reestablished from the Carolinas and Georgia to Tennessee and Kentucky.[15]

Between 1871 and March 1873, Molly and Donald were stationed at five different military posts in the Southeast. In April 1873, the couple was ordered to report to Yankton in the Dakota Territory. Members of the Seventh Cavalry were to meet at the location and move as a unit to Fort Rice. From there, they would serve as a field military escort for the Northern Pacific Railroad survey crew expedition.

Molly and Donald separated at Fort Rice. The post lacked adequate housing for officers' wives, and the couple thought it was best Molly return to her parents' home. The pair would remain apart until September 21, 1873, when they met at Fort Abraham Lincoln.[16]

Life at Fort Abraham Lincoln was idyllic for Molly and Donald. They had an active social life. For Molly, there were sewing bees with Elizabeth Custer, Nettie Smith, and Annie Yates. For Donald, it was hunting trips and cards. Together they enjoyed dinner parties and picnics with Custer and his favorite people.

In the spring of 1874, Molly traveled east to retrieve her sister who couldn't wait to visit again. Donald was on hand to meet his wife and sister-in-law when they arrived in Bismarck. Katherine described in her diary the touching scene between her sister and brother-in-law when they were reunited. "Suddenly from behind a wooden pillar, stepped the tall, lithe figure of an army officer in uniform, wearing a forage cap which bore the number 7, and a pair of shoulder straps showing the insignia of a First Lieutenant," Katherine wrote. "'There's Donald,' exclaimed Molly as excitedly as though they had been separated a month. He hurried toward

The officers and their wives enjoy a quiet evening at the Custers' home at Fort
Lincoln in 1875, with Margaret Calhoun playing the piano.
COURTESY OF THE NATIONAL PARK SERVICE, LITTLE BIGHORN BATTLEFIELD NATIONAL MONUMENT

us, and, as I looked into his strong, purposeful face and kindly dark eyes,
I suddenly knew that Molly was a very lucky woman."[17]

In early 1875, Molly's sister married a well-respected lieutenant
with the Seventh Cavalry and friend of General Custer and Elizabeth's,
twenty-eight-year-old Frank Gibson. Molly, Elizabeth, Maggie Calhoun,
and Annie Yates helped plan the wedding. Several members of the Seventh Cavalry and their wives attended the ceremony. Donald gave away
the bride.[18]

Shortly after the wedding, Molly and Donald traveled to Shreveport, Louisiana, where the first lieutenant was to report for duty. The
Shreveport area of northwestern Louisiana was one of the most lawless
parts of the country following Secession in the 1870s. Unruly mobs were
attacking Black Americans, and the military was there to assist local law
enforcement agencies to restore and keep order.[19]

Charades at Fort Lincoln
rom left to right, Maggie Custer, Tom Custer, and Mrs. Custer
as "Flora McFlimsey with Nothing to Wear."

A game of charades provided a great deal of entertainment for General Custer, Elizabeth, his officers, and their wives; from left to right: Margaret Calhoun, Tom Custer, and Elizabeth Custer.
COURTESY OF THE STATE HISTORICAL SOCIETY OF NORTH DAKOTA, A4379-00001

By April 1876, the McIntoshes were ordered to return to Fort Abraham Lincoln. Molly was reunited with her sister and her new husband at the post, and for a few weeks all was as it had been. The McIntoshes and the Gibsons joined the Custers and the others in the general's inner circle of friends for what would be their last get-together.

Katherine confessed in her memoirs the sense of dread and foreboding that overcame her during the days leading up to the Seventh Cavalry marching to Montana. She'd had a premonition of something tragic happening to Donald but did not share her feelings with Molly. "It was all so

Seventh Cavalry officers and their wives photographed at Fort Lincoln in 1875; Lieutenant Donald McIntosh is seated at the far right, with Molly standing next to him.

inexplicable, so silly, I told myself angrily," Katherine wrote in her autobiography, "yet that sinister brooding bit deeper and deeper into my being."[20]

Letters Donald wrote Molly from the field gave no indication there was anything out of the ordinary with the expedition upon which the Seventh Cavalry had embarked. Husband and wife believed they would be together again before the summer ended.

Donald's letter to Molly of May 20, 1876, provides one such example:

My dear Honey,

This is the fourth day from Lincoln and only forty-five miles from there. We have been having very wet weather, and yesterday afternoon it stormed fearfully. The thunder going off like a cannon apparently just over our heads, then came torrents of rain and hail as big as walnuts. My horse, Shakespeare, became nervous stricken, but only for a second, for dismounting and patting him on the neck and speaking to him quietly reassured him until it was over.[21]

Nearly everybody got wet. Some thoroughly so. My boots were full of water, but this morning I got up feeling no effects.

I don't know what this expedition is called officially. Some call it the Yellowstone Expedition, when others say its official designation is the Sioux Expedition. It don't [sic] matter much, I suppose, except that letters might miscarry, for there are two other expeditions on against the Sioux. A courier brought this mail from Lincoln to our camp yesterday. If you address [the letters] as I told you in one of my last letters, I don't think there will be anything miscarried.

I am enjoying the trip, as I generally do after getting started, and the duty in camp is nothing at all outside what I would have to do anywhere in the company. There being no officer of the day business and much to the delight of the second. . . .

All are vowing by the great horn spoon!* *. . . Custer came in with his regiment. Reno on the right wing with 1 company. Benteen on the left wing with same number of companies. I am in Benteen's wing, so are Godfrey, Weir, Moylan, and French. Strange to say Weir has not drank [sic] anything since I came here with the Seventh. He seems*

---

* An Irish term; an oath, or, at least, a way to make a statement sound emphatic.

very quiet, keeping in his own tent much of the time. There is no sutler along, which I think is a good thing every way.

A courier brought this mail from Lincoln yesterday and in it your letter of the 10th. The same courier delivers in about half an hour and we have just got into camp. I only have time to write you this much. I don't know whether this will be the last courier or not. I'll write every chance I get.

. . . In most respects am in better fix than I have ever been on an expedition. I am well, thoroughly so, and in the course of two or three weeks will be in condition for most any raid on horseback. . . . I have got my trunk along so that I have everything with me that I can possibly need for cold or hot weather.

Love to everybody in the house . . . Kisses and all my love.

Your dearest husband,

Donald McIntosh

P.S. Colonel Gibbon who is coming down the Yellowstone with our expedition reported no Indians. My opinion is that we won't see any either.[22]

The letter Donald wrote Molly on June 22, 1876, was the last he would write.

I heard late tonight that a mail run would leave today by a noon boat. The wind is and has been blowing so hard that it is difficult to do anything. . . . Everybody is well. I am well. There is nothing new. No Indians have been seen as yet. The wind is blowing so, and besides that I have so much to attend to I'll have to stop.[23]

All our wagons were left behind some days ago, and we have nothing but pack mules to carry our things. I wrote you about a week ago, but the mail in which it went fell overboard somewhere down the river and everything got so wet that the letters had to be redirected and stamped. I also wrote at the same time to H. A. Town, Supt. of the Northern Pacific Railroad, Brainard, D. T., asking him to send you a pass for yourself and a servant.

Nobody knows yet when the expedition will get back. Probably Gen. Terry will be able to decide upon that subject after this scout. I wrote you in my last [letter] that I would come back to look after the business if there was a chance, but that if there was no chance for me, I would not go.

All our things are stored with the company property at Lincoln. Love to everybody.

    I am your devoted husband,

    Donald McIntosh[24]

When news reached the fort about the death of Custer's command at the Little Bighorn, Katherine grieved with her sister over the loss of Donald.[25] The letter Katherine received from her husband, written on July 4, 1876, explained in detail all that had happened.

My dear Wife,

    We have just been notified that mail will leave at seven o'clock tonight, so I have time to write you all the particulars.[26]

    We left the boat at the mouth of the Rosebud at noon on the twenty-second. The boat came up the mouth of the Big Horn with General Terry, and crossed Gibbon's command which was to connect with us on the Little Big Horn River. On the twenty-third, we struck an Indian trail, only two days old, so we marched night and day at trot and gallop with occasional short halts so, of course, the men and horses became exhausted for the need of rest and food, but still we went pushing and crowding along.

    At ten a.m. on the twenty-fifth, we halted, and officers' call was sounded, and after we assembled, General Custer said the command had been discovered by the Indians, and our scout had reported the village about fifteen miles off. He then said the companies would resume march in the order that the company commanders reported them ready. Well, as it happened, Benteen was the first to report, so when the forward call was sounded our H company was leading the column.

As we marched along through the heat I could not but recall the rather odd talk we had with Custer on the evening of the twenty second. When officers' call was sounded, we assembled at his bivouac and squatted in groups about his cot. He told us that he expected to encounter at least a thousand Indians, and that all precautions for a long campaign must be taken. He said that until further orders no trumpet calls would be sounded except in an emergency. General Terry had offered him the additional force of the Second Cavalry which he had declined, confident that the Seventh could handle the matter alone. He also declined the offer of Gatling guns because they might hamper our movements through such rugged country. We were cautioned to husband our mules and ammunition and, finally, he asked all officers to make any suggestions to him at any time. This struck us all as the strangest part of the meeting, for you know how dominant and self-reliant he always was, and we left him with a queer sort of depression. McIntosh, Wallace, Godfrey and I walked back to our tents together, and finally Wallace said—"I believe General Custer is going to be killed."

"Why?" asked Godfrey.

"Because I never heard him talk that way before—that is, asking the advice of anyone."

This was going through my mind during the five miles of march and then we saw clouds of dust about ten miles ahead of us, so the column again halted, and battalions were formed of three companies each, commanded by Reno, Yates, [and] Keogh. Benteen's battalion, which was composed of H, D, and K companies, was sent to the left about five miles to see if the Indians were trying to escape up the valley of the Little Big Horn, after which we were to hurry and rejoin the command as quickly as possible.

We never saw Custer after that. He went on with the balance of the command and, when he got in sight of the village, he ordered Reno, with companies A, G, and M, to cross the Little Big Horn and open the fight, while he kept to the right with companies C, E, F, I, and L, and would attack the village in another place, and all this time Tom McDougall with B company was about three miles in our rear, bringing up the pack mules. When we got within two miles of the village, Benteen got a note from Cooke, which ran thus—"Come on—big village—be quick—bring packs." We didn't wait for the packs as we felt pretty sure no Indians had passed our rear.[27]

When we reached the battleground, we found utter confusion.

. . . The Indians left their village to fight Custer and fought dismounted. The officers of Gibbon's command know this Crow Indian and say he is a truthful man. In our seven companies they killed and wounded about one-hundred-twelve men and two officers.

On the twenty-seventh I buried McIntosh, and his grave is nicely marked. . . . Poor Molly—her heart will be completely broken.[28]

In 1876, Elizabeth Custer wrote to a friend to explain why Molly refused to see anyone while grieving her husband's death. "A wounded thing must hide," she explained to him.[29]

This is exactly what Molly did, hiding herself away at her mother's home. The sure knowledge that life would go on without Donald, that time was only stopped for her, undid her completely for several years.

General Custer and Elizabeth eating at camp headquarters near Fort Hays, Kansas; their friends, the Seventh Cavalry officers and their wives, are nearby.
COURTESY OF THE NATIONAL PARK SERVICE, LITTLE BIGHORN BATTLEFIELD NATIONAL MONUMENT, LIBI-00019_00496, PHOTOGRAPHED BY W. J. PHILLIPS, CIRCA 1869

Officers' quarters at Fort Lincoln, North Dakota
COURTESY OF THE STATE HISTORICAL SOCIETY OF NORTH DAKOTA, A4362-00001

GENERAL CUSTER'S DEATH STRUGGLE.
The Battle of the Little Big Horn.

Drawing of General Custer and members of the Seventh Cavalry at the Battle of the Little Bighorn
COURTESY OF THE LIBRARY OF CONGRESS, LC-USZ62-48

CHAPTER FIVE

Left Behind

On Saturday, May 27, 1876, Henrietta "Nettie" Smith, her good friend Elizabeth Custer, and several other soldiers' wives made their way to the steamship *Far West*, docked in the waters near Fort Abraham Lincoln. They were excited and filled with purpose. They planned to persuade the ship's captain, Grant Marsh, to transport them up the Missouri to the Yellowstone River, near where their husbands were camped.[1]

The wives of the Seventh Cavalry officers had met with their spouses in the field before, some living in tents with them while they performed their duties, so the request wasn't out of the ordinary. When the troops had marched away from the fort a mere nine days prior, the good-byes had been emotional and touching. Nettie Smith, who had been married to First Lieutenant Algernon Smith for more than nine years, was desperate to see him again. A sense of fear and foreboding over his safety had overtaken her, and letters he had written assuring her he was fine could not convince her he was well.

Far West crew members welcomed the women aboard the vessel, and as per the custom, Captain Marsh ordered

Captain Algernon Smith
COURTESY OF THE DENVER PUBLIC LIBRARY, SPECIAL COLLECTIONS

a meal prepared for them. Nettie, Elizabeth, and the other wives were escorted to the ship's dining room where they were served "as dainty a luncheon as the larder of the boat could afford." Elizabeth requested the captain join them, and he reluctantly did so. He was busy preparing the steamship to rendezvous with the Seventh Cavalry. He and his thirty-man crew were loading the vessel with food, ammunition, and other supplies the troops would need. There wasn't a moment to spare.[2]

After listening patiently to the officers' wives' request, Captain Marsh explained that in the best of circumstances, "he did not wish to be burdened with many passengers for whose safety and comfort he would be responsible." He went on to inform the women that the anticipated voyage to the Yellowstone River would be "both dangerous and uncomfortable."

This revelation did not cause the women to change their minds about their objective. They believed their place was with their husbands, wherever they were and whatever peril might lie ahead. Captain Marsh com-

Steamboat *Far West*
COURTESY OF THE DENVER PUBLIC LIBRARY, SPECIAL COLLECTIONS

plimented their devotion to their loved ones but, nonetheless, refused to take them on the voyage. He suggested they wait for the steamboat *Josephine*. *Josephine* was scheduled to travel from Bismarck to the Yellowstone River in the coming weeks and was much more suitable for polite passengers than the *Far West*. The women didn't want to wait for another boat and appealed again to Captain Marsh. There was no changing his mind.[3]

Realizing there was nothing left to do, Nettie and Elizabeth made their way back to the Custers' quarters, gravely dismayed. "It is infinitely worse to be left behind," Elizabeth later wrote, "a prey to all the horrors of imagining what may be happening to the one you love. You slowly eat your heart out with anxiety, and to endure such suspense is simply the hardest of all trials that come to the soldier's wife."[4]

Nettie Smith nearly collapsed when she was informed of her husband's death. She later told friends it was as if she herself had died at that very moment. She didn't know if she could bring herself to attend the burial of her husband's remains at Fort Leavenworth on August 4, 1877. When she had left the sad party of widows in Chicago in July 1876 to travel to her family's home in Herkimer County, New York, she believed then she could only bear to honor her husband's memory at the place where they had met and married.

A poem written for Nettie and the other widows of the Seventh Cavalry aptly describes the deep sorrow she felt over losing Algernon, the sentiment ringing true for her years after his death.[5]

> His country took him from my side.
> I had no will to bid him stay,
> though I had been my soldier's bride.
> Had happier fate been ours that day.
> He died a glorious death—ah, yes!
> His praises ring through all the land;
> but, oh, for one fond, sweet caress,
> one pressure of his loving hand!
> They tell me of heroic deeds
> and strive to cheer me with his praise;
> my heart with keener sorrow bleeds,
> remembering all those happier days.

For what is praise of blame to me who wait,
and know I wait in vain,
the joy that nevermore can be.
To wake me from this dream of pain.[6]

Nettie and Algernon had been born eight months apart in Newport,
New York. He was born on September 17, 1842, and Nettie, on May 9,
1843. In 1862, Algernon enlisted in the 117th New York Volunteers. He
proved himself to be a good soldier and was rapidly promoted through
the ranks. At the end of the Civil War, he was mustered out of the volunteer service with the rank of major. His soldierly qualities attracted the
attention of military officials, and he was given a commission as second
lieutenant in the Seventh Regular Cavalry. He was soon promoted to the
rank of first lieutenant and brevet-captain. In the active and often delicate duties which had been assigned to his regiment, he was recognized
by his superior officers as being gallant and efficient. As the quartermaster of the Black Hills Expedition in 1874, he commanded an immense
transportation and supply train and discharged the usual duties of the
occasion in a manner which elicited general commendation.[7]

Nettie and Algernon met while attending school and were married
on October 10, 1867, in Newport, New York, at the home of her parents,
Hezekiah and Mary Bowen. Friends and family noted that the Smiths
"possessed fine senses of humor and were well liked by everyone [with
whom] they came in contact."

Among those charmed by their personalities were George and Elizabeth Custer. The four met at Fort Hays, Kansas, in April 1869. The
Custers invited the Smiths to join them and the other members of their
inner circle to camp on Big Creek near Fort Hays. The men in the group
hunted and fished, and the wives sewed and read aloud to one another.
Nettie had a natural talent for administering first aid to anyone in the
party who injured himself. Some of the Custer clan playfully referred
to her as "nurse." Algernon also had a nickname. There were two men
named Smith in the Seventh Cavalry, and, to distinguish the officers
from one another, one was called "Salt," and the younger one, Algernon,
was called "Fresh."[8]

Nettie and Algernon enjoyed their life together and the time spent on the plains. An article in the September 12, 1869, edition of the *Ellsworth Daily Evening Democrat* described one of the memorable excursions across Kansas in which they took part.

About half past eight the train pulled out from Hays City up a pretty steep grade with all the party on the lookout for buffalo or any other game worthy of their attention. This, judging from the shooting, included prairie dogs, many villages of which we passed on the road. After the first station (which was merely a water tank) several of the party took seats upon the top of the engine, which gave a fine view of the country, and the first show at any buffalo which might present themselves.[9]

The aforesaid buffalo, I will say here, failed signally in presenting themselves. After a while, the position was rendered pleasanter by the company of one or two ladies of the party, who overcame their fears sufficiently to "take the lead in rushing o'er the grassy plains." One is much surprised in riding over such a seemingly level surface to find such steep grades, and so many of them as are found between Hays City and Sheridan.

The train reached the latter place about two p.m. to find quite a little town nestled down in a hollow on the plains, without a tree in sight, and the sun beating down most fiercely. After a rest of about an hour, which gave the excursionist an opportunity to move around, get some dinner and view the fine expanse of country (from [a] hollow), the train started back for Hays City, in order to reach it before dark. The trains never run after dark in this part of the country.

About half past eight we reached Hays City and found ambulances and wagons in waiting to convey the excursionists over to the "Post" nearby, where quarters had been provided for many of them, which most of the party availed themselves of. Many of the party were entertained by Captain Kimball, Quartermaster of the Post. Everything in their power was done by Captain and Mrs. Kimball to entertain the excursionists, and they enjoyed a most delightful evening. Colonel Gibson, Commander of the Post, had made provision for their accommodation for the night and breakfast, and wagons for the gentlemen, and ambulances for the ladies to go out upon the prairie to witness the grand buffalo hunt, which was to take place that day, given in honor of the visit of Lord Paget and Lord Waterpark, two young English noblemen who had come West in quest of sport and hunting.

In accordance with an invitation extended by General S. D. Sturgis to Mr. Wheeler, of the New York Times, *and to the undersigned before we left Sheridan, we reported to him immediately upon arriving at the post. Very comfortable quarters were provided us at the house of Captain Kimball, and in the morning, we went over [to] the camp of the Seventh Cavalry, located about a mile and half from the Post, in a beautiful triangle formed by the Big Timber, on the banks of which it is located. We breakfasted with General Sturgis, at whose hospitable board we met his son and Lords Paget and Waterpark, whom we found very agreeable and very anxious to chase the buffalo.*

After a hearty breakfast we were furnished a horse, belt and pistols, and the party started toward the buffalo range. Before leaving the camp of the 7th, the party was joined by the main body of the excursionists in the conveyances provided for them by the kindness of the officers, and then moved forward. In the lead were General Custer, the English Gentlemen, officers of the 7th Cavalry, and some of the excursion party, who had been mounted.

About noon we reached a beautiful spot on the banks of the "Smoky," where our camp was to be pitched, which was to be the base of the future operations. After a rest of half an hour, the scouts reported buffalo about three miles to the east, and the party remounted and moved to the front. While the horsemen had been resting, the party in vehicles had been allowed to roam on so as to be as near the spot as possible when the grand dash was made. About half past two, the party came on a herd of buffalo, and the dash was made in full view. A prettier sight I never saw. . . .

During the first day's sport, about forty animals were killed and the party returned to their "Smoky" camp pretty well tired out. The excursionists, after a short rest and refreshments, returned to Hays City, and left for the East about half past nine o'clock, I believe.

After dinner we spent the time very pleasantly in conversation and such sports as are in vogue in the camp. Here we were joined by Mrs. General Custer, Mrs. Captain Smith, and Mrs. Godfrey, and, of course, the presence of ladies made a pleasant and pretty scene still pleasanter and prettier. Very early, however, the camp became quiet, for the hunters were tired and needed rest and refreshments for the morrow's hunt.[10]

By early 1872, the Custers and the Smiths were sharing a large home at their new post in Elizabethtown, Kentucky. Nettie and Elizabeth alternated housekeeping chores each week. Lieutenant Smith, General Custer, and the other members of the Seventh Cavalry spent their days helping local law enforcement keep the peace in the area by breaking up illicit distilleries and controlling the carpetbaggers and the Ku Klux Klan. Nettie and Elizabeth hosted tea parties and made clothing with the new sewing machine Custer had bought his wife in Louisville.[11]

Although the Smiths and the Custers got along well, sharing a home did prove to be frustrating for Nettie and Algernon. Algernon felt Custer undermined his authority over the regiment he commanded, and Nettie believed Elizabeth interfered in their marriage at times.[12] Elizabeth was aware of the times she overstepped. She wrote about a particular instance in her memoirs *Tenting on the Plains.*

"I recall the chagrin I felt on the plains one day, when one of our Seventh Cavalry officers, with whom we had long been intimately associated, one of whom people called 'Fresh Smith' or 'Smithie,' for short, came to his wife to get her to put on his coat," Elizabeth explained. "I said something in bantering tones of his plains life making him look on his wife as the Indian looks upon the squaw and tried to rouse her to rebellion. There was a small blaze, a sudden scintillation from a pair of feminine eyes [belonging to Nettie], that warned me of the wrath to come.[13]

"The captain accepted my banter, threw himself into the saddle, laughed back the advantage of this new order of things, where a man had a combination, in his wife, of servant and companion, and tore out of sight, leaving me to settle accounts with the flushed madam. She told me, what I never knew, and perhaps might not even now, but for the outburst of the moment, that in the [Civil] [W]ar 'Smithie' had received a wound that shattered his shoulder, and though his arm was narrowly saved from amputation, he never raised it again, except a few inches. As for putting on his coat, it was [an] impossibility."[14]

The Smiths, along with the rest of the Seventh Cavalry, were transferred from Kentucky to Yankton in the Dakota Territory in February 1873. When they arrived, the weather was harsh, and the conditions at Fort Yankton less than inviting, but the people who resided in the area were warm and welcoming. On April 17, the citizens held a ball in honor of the Seventh Cavalry. Nettie and Algernon were excited to take part in the festivities.

According to the May 4, 1873, edition of the *Sioux City Journal*,

> *The Reception Ball was held at Stone's Hall, which was profusely decorated with flags, the wall being completely hidden from view by starry banners arranged in the most attractive and tasteful manner, while the ceiling was hung with like emblems gracefully festooned.*[15]
>
> *These striking ornaments with the bright, full dress uniforms of the military gentlemen present were sufficient to call to mind Byron's famous "Battle of Waterloo" ["The Eve of Waterloo"], from which the* Journal *in its account makes appropriate and liberal quotations. There were present about one hundred twenty couples embracing the leading professional and commercial men of Yankton with their ladies, while the officers were fully represented.*
>
> *Among those who participated there was a unanimous expression that they had never enjoyed an entertainment more thoroughly.*[16]

From Yankton, the Smiths moved to Fort Rice with the Seventh Cavalry. No sooner had they arrived than the cavalry was ordered to accompany a survey crew with the Northern Pacific Railroad along the uncompleted portion of their road extending westward. The Yellowstone Expedition, as it was called, began on June 20, 1873.

Nettie was anxious about Algernon leaving. She feared he might encounter Native Americans who resented their presence in the region and would do whatever they could to drive away the troops. An article in the June 20, 1873, edition of the *Star Tribune* reported that "no trouble is expected with the Indians as they are not of a class of combatants that hit a head whenever they see it. Discretion they regard as the better part of valor when there is a large body of troops in the immediate vicinity."[17]

Algernon promised to write Nettie as often as he could to reassure her that he was well and had come to no harm. Captain Smith wrote his wife frequently, sharing with her the daily activities of a soldier's life in the field. "Our friendly allies, the Indian scouts, are especially enthusiastic about this tour and with the prospect of leading the advance and discovering the lurking places of their implacable enemies, the hostile Sioux, who had avowed their intention of annoying the expedition," Algernon wrote his wife on July 22, 1873. "They had a grand pow-wow the night of their departure, keeping it up till near morning, with howls and ceremonies peculiar to their character. Whether it was conducted under the influence of too much whiskey, which they had by some means procured, or of anticipations of a little exciting warfare and the lively incidents of a campaign, or both combined, we are not sure. All were ready to exchange the life in camp for the excitement, the hardships, and pleasures of the month."[18]

Three months would pass before Nettie saw her husband again. The two were reunited at Fort Abraham Lincoln on September 21, 1873. The Smiths enjoyed their life at the post. Surrounded by their friends and colleagues, the couple spent many evenings and weekends in the company of the Custers and the others close to George and Elizabeth.[19]

Nettie and Algernon were separated again in July 1874. This time the Seventh Cavalry was to take part in the Black Hills Expedition. Nettie couldn't hide her anxiety over the thought of Algernon leaving on another potentially dangerous trek. Many of the other "daughters of the regiment" were also feeling the same concern.[20] Newspaper articles that filtered into the post added to their worries. One report Nettie read and pasted in the scrapbook she kept was the July 4, 1874, edition of the *Inter Ocean*.

Officers' wives pose for a photograph on the porch and steps of Elizabeth and George Custer's quarters at Fort Lincoln.
COURTESY OF THE STATE HISTORICAL SOCIETY OF NORTH DAKOTA, C3567-00001

The Black Hills Expedition left here yesterday morning, under command of General George A. Custer, General Forsyth, and General M. S. Tilson commanding the wings. The column consists of ten companies of the Seventh Cavalry, three companies of infantry, 100 Indian scouts under command of the famous Bloody Knife, and a battery of Gatling guns. The train consists of 150 wagons and carries supplies for sixty days. The party will probably be gone until the 1st of October, making a thorough exploration of the legendary region of the Black Hills and establishing a site for the building of a fort and trading post there.[21]

It is probable that a strong resistance will be made by the Indians, as startling rumors are constantly arriving at this place of the gathering of the different Sioux tribes under Sitting Bull about seventy

Black Hills Expedition
COURTESY OF THE STATE HISTORICAL SOCIETY OF NORTH DAKOTA, A5359-00001

miles to the south. An Indian missionary came to this post a few days since the information that the Indians intended to contest every foot of the march, and he begged General Custer to give up the expedition to save bloodshed. The treaty reserves the right to the United States to pass through and explore all the contested territory, and General Custer is prepared to enforce that right. A severe conflict may be expected before many days.[22]

Algernon and Nettie corresponded with one another daily. In late July 1874, she received a letter he had written about his difficulties accurately firing his weapon. She attributed his trouble to his arm that had been injured in the Civil War. She felt badly for him, but he made light of the situation. "This is the note sent to General Custer after a disappointing showing on the range," Algernon shared with Nettie. "A raw recruit at practicing hitting a target. . . . Never could hit even the outer rim. I am perfectly disgusted. I wish you'd give me another gun, General, for this one shoots crooked as hell."[23]

Custer and his command returned to Fort Abraham Lincoln from the Black Hills Expedition on August 30, 1874. The Smiths resumed their life together at the post, continuing the same routine they had established before Algernon left on the expedition. They participated in all social events organized by the Custers and made plans for life beyond the military. Algernon's sister lived in Utica, New York, with her husband, Dr. H. Holmes. The Holmes family had extended an offer to Nettie and Algernon to move into one of the homes on their estate once Algernon retired from the army. The Smiths spent several hours discussing the invitation and considering what line of work would be best for Algernon to pursue.[24]

Dreams for a happy-ever-after ended in late June 1876 when Captain Smith was killed at the Battle of the Little Bighorn. Nettie was crushed by the news and sought every means possible to keep the memory of her deceased husband in the forefront of her mind. She collected every newspaper article about the tragedy and refused to talk about him in the past tense. Among the notices about Algernon's death was one from the *Buffalo Weekly Courier*, dated July 12, 1876.[25]

Among the gallant officers of the Seventh Cavalry who fell with their commander on the bloody field at Little Big Horn, was First Lieutenant and Brevet-Captain Algernon E. Smith, whose home was in Herkimer County, this state, and who has many friends in this city. . . .

In the last fatal charge of General Custer's command, Captain Smith was, as usual, near his chivalrous young commander, and their bodies were found lying near each other. Captain Smith was a brave and capable officer, a warm and unselfish friend, and courteous gentleman.[26]

Life for Nettie in Newport, New York, was trying without Algernon. For a while, she shut herself off from everyone. She added clippings, letters, and poems to the book of mementos made to hold the recollections of her husband. She clung to the watch fob retrieved from his back pocket before he was placed in a shallow grave at the battle site. The gold horse watch fob found in his trousers had been overlooked by the

Bones of the horses that perished at the Battle of the Little Bighorn
COURTESY OF THE LIBRARY OF CONGRESS, LC-DIG-PPMSCA-15946

Indians taking items from the deceased soldiers, and had made its way back to Nettie. She eventually passed the fob along to one of Algernon's best friends, Lieutenant Frank Gibson. According to Frank's daughter's memoirs, her father had always admired the watch fob. In the evenings around the campfire, Frank and Algernon would tease one another about what would happen to the item if he died. "Gib, if I'm killed first, I will [get] the fob to you, and, if you go first, I get your bloodstone ring," Algernon told Frank. Frank wore the fob until the day he passed away in January 1919.[27]

During the first few months after Algernon died, Nettie exchanged letters with Elizabeth Custer, expressing how lost she felt since losing her husband. "I happened onto a note my sweet left for me shortly after we were married. He called me his 'most amiable and accomplished wife' and begged me to always remember how much he adored me. I'll forever be grief stricken without him."[28]

The Chicago, Rock Island and Pacific Railroad delivered the remains of five officers of the Seventh Cavalry to the Union Depot at Fort Leavenworth on August 3, 1877. Nettie Smith was on hand as her husband's remains were offloaded and placed in a carriage. His coffin was placed in the post chapel along with the others. The following day, their bodies were laid to rest at the National Cemetery. After the religious ceremonies, troops fired a salute over the soldiers' graves. The remains of the departed were lowered into the ground and the caskets covered with wreaths.[29]

The thousands who had come to pay their respects slowly left the cemetery at the conclusion of the service. Nettie stayed behind to remember the man she loved and leave flowers at Algernon's final resting place.

CHAPTER SIX

One So Noble

SOBBING UNCONTROLLABLY, TWENTY-EIGHT-YEAR-OLD ELIZA PORTER stood in front of her husband First Lieutenant James Porter's headstone at the Strong Village Cemetery in Strong, Maine. Her five-month-old son, James Francis, was fast asleep in her arms, blissfully unaware that his father had died. The Porters' oldest son, five-year-old David, darted around the grave markers, chasing butterflies. He could not fully understand the sad circumstances.

Like General George Custer's other officers, First Lieutenant Porter was killed on June 25, 1876. His body was never recovered nor identified. The lining of his buckskin coat was found in an Indian camp days after the Battle of the Little Bighorn. The soldiers who came upon the bloody garment noticed a bullet hole in the coat. They speculated that the bullet had torn through the lieutenant's back and into his heart.[1]

The funeral exercises commemorative of the services and death of a gallant officer were held on September 10, 1876. A large concourse

Lieutenant James Porter
CLASS ALBUM COLLECTION, US MILITARY
ACADEMY LIBRARY

95

of people from every portion of the county had attended the memorial. According to historical records, the services held for First Lieutenant Porter at the Congregational Church in Strong were simple and solemn. A canopy was constructed in the rear of the pulpit, and, against the wall, American flags were tastefully festooned and intertwined with white muslin and black crepe.

Beneath that, in evergreen, appeared the name of "Lieutenant J. E. Porter." On the table in front of the pulpit lay his regulation cap and two of his sabers. The sabers were crossed with the points extending up to either end of a Bible resting on a stand; between them was suspended a large picture of Porter. The rest of the church was decorated with flowers brought by mourners who wanted to pay tribute to the valor and sacrifice of the fallen soldier.[2]

Reverend Trafton presided over the service and offered the following address to First Lieutenant Porter's family and friends: "No words of ours can soften the grief of those so sadly stricken by the death of one so noble and promising, and no eulogy we can pronounce would reach the eloquence of his deeds. Patriot, soldier, farewell; thy labors and privations are ended, but thy fame is but begun."

At the conclusion of the funeral service, Eliza found herself at her husband's marble headstone, reflecting on their life together. She would later share in a letter to Elizabeth Custer that in that moment, standing at James's grave marker "recalling the horrors of the torture he most assuredly suffered," an "awful hollowness engulfed" her "mind, body, and soul."[3]

Eliza Frances Westcott Porter was born in December 1849 in Warwick, Rhode Island. Her family was one of the oldest in New England, having arrived in America from Yeovil, England, in 1677. Eliza's father was a civil engineer and farmer. She was an educated woman who excelled in math. She was barely nineteen when she met twenty-one-year-old James Ezekiel Porter. Porter, the son of a prominent family in Strong, Maine, was a student at West Point at the time, having attended the Maine Seminary and the Seminary in Norwich. He graduated from West Point in 1869, sixteenth in a class of thirty-nine students. Two months after

James graduated from the US Military Academy, he was commissioned as a second lieutenant and assigned to the Seventh Cavalry.[4]

The Porters were stationed at Fort Hays, Kansas, in September 1869, and it was there the pair met George and Elizabeth Custer. Lieutenant Porter and Eliza got along well with his commanding officer and wife and quickly became a part of the Custers' close-knit circle of friends. Not long after making the Custers' acquaintance, the newlyweds joined Custer and the other officers and their wives on an outing not far from Hays City. The excursion made the front page of the *Daily Kansas Tribune* on September 9, 1869:

> *A large party, consisting of two English noblemen, Lord Waterpark and Lord Paget, with Generals Custer and Sturgis and several officers of the Seventh Cavalry, left the camp of the latter at an early hour this morning to participate in a grand buffalo hunt. Several ladies accompanied the party . . .*[5]
>
> *A messenger has just returned and reports the hunt was progressing finely, the party having been out only five hours and killed over forty buffalo, the English noblemen killing two each. A large wager had been made by the Englishmen with friends at home upon the fact of killing at least one buffalo. The party proposes staying out three or four days longer, and they evidently intend enjoying themselves. The band of the Seventh Cavalry accompanied the party.*[6]

By 1871, the Porters were living at an army post in Yorkville, South Carolina. Lieutenant Porter had command of the Seventh Cavalry's Company C, whose job it was to work with local authorities to keep the Ku Klux Klan under control. The Klan's crimes across the interior of the state had reached such an extreme level that the government needed to send in troops to stop the violence being perpetrated on Black Americans. Both Porter and Eliza were appalled at the actions of the Klan. Eliza spoke out against the group at church socials and at various women's club meetings. Porter and his troops were dispatched to a variety of locations within South Carolina to apprehend KKK members who lynched free men.[7]

Lieutenant Porter received accolades for his fine work from his superiors and was held in high regard by the townspeople he met while on duty. On May 31, 1871, Porter's presence was happily reported in the *Fairfield Herald* of Winnsboro, South Carolina:[8]

> *We have had the pleasure of Lieutenant Porter's acquaintance and visits to our office, and find him to be a pleasant, social and fair-minded gentleman. We hope our citizens will extend to him the courtesies due a gentleman.*
>
> *Lieutenant J. E. Porter, of Troop C, Seventh Cavalry, with a detachment of twenty men, left this post on Friday last to garrison the town of Winnsboro. This movement is in pursuance of the President's program to station troops at every point in South Carolina, Georgia, and North Carolina, where there seems to be probability of the vote being against the Republican party in 1872.*
>
> *We have had the opportunity of being acquainted with Lieutenant Porter during his stay at this place and take pleasure in commending him to the people of Fairfield as a fair-minded and cultivated gentleman.*[9]

Porter was excelling in his duties as an army officer, and life at home for him and Eliza was going well, too. On October 13, 1871, the couple welcomed their first child, a son they named David Arthur.[10]

The Porters remained in South Carolina until April 1872. Along with other members of his company, James continued to fight against prejudice and to do battle with the KKK. According to the April 27, 1872, edition of the *Yorkville Enquirer*, "The presence of Lieutenant Porter, his troops, and their families are a source of interest and pleasure to the town. . . . The officers are gentlemen of refinement and culture, and we doubt not that they would impartially discharge their duty in every emergency that might arise."[11]

From South Carolina, the Porters were transferred to Memphis, Tennessee, along with other divisions within the Seventh Cavalry.[12] Their stay in Tennessee was brief. After a few weeks, they were off to Fort Rice in the Dakota Territory. As Porter marched with his fellow soldiers to their new post, Eliza and David followed along by train with the other officers' wives. The time the Porters spent apart was "torturous," Eliza later wrote to her husband. During his absence, she bonded with Elizabeth Custer and the other officers' wives, who were all experiencing life alone in the cold, hostile environment. "I feel certain I could better endure the seemingly unending snowfall if you were here beside me, my dear," Eliza wrote James on Friday, March 28, 1873. "Time stands still when you are gone. I am sustained daily by our little one. I shudder to think what our life would be without the thought of you returning to the place you most desperately belong."[13]

By mid-April, the Porters had reunited. On April 17, the pair left their little boy in the care of a sitter and attended a ball hosted by the citizens of Yankton. The grand event was held at the public hall in town, and all members of the Seventh Cavalry were invited. The memory

Sketch of Fort Rice in the Dakota Territory, 1870
COURTESY OF THE STATE HISTORICAL SOCIETY OF NORTH DAKOTA, B0764-00001

of the festive evening the Porters spent together would sustain them through another separation that began in late June, when Custer and his command left Fort Rice on the Yellowstone Expedition. The expedition, comprised of 1,900 men and 250 wagons, was under the command of Major General David Stanley. Custer oversaw the cavalry.[14]

The expedition was one of five engineering surveys undertaken by the Northern Pacific Railroad into Montana's Yellowstone Valley and western Dakota Territory to establish a final route for the railroad.

Eliza and James wrote one another often while they were apart. James sent letters to his wife describing the setting he and the others were exploring. "The Yellowstone is certainly one of the most beautiful rivers in the world," James informed his wife on July 20, 1873. "Now the river is quite full and averages over 1,000 feet in width, with over four feet of water on the bars. I'm sure the rate of the current is six miles an hour, and for some reason appears to the eye swifter than that rate would indicate. The water is quite clear and produces some of the finest drinking water.[15]

"The valley of the Yellowstone is upon an average about two miles in width, and the hills bounding the valley average 300 feet in height. This is the area where they have found coal. One cut bluff of coal was observed eight miles above the Powder River which measured 16 feet of the exposed face, and its horizontal area seemed immense. The grass is rank and of the finest varieties. Timber does not become abundant till we reach the mouth of the Tongue River, from which point heavy bodies of cotton wood continually line the low banks on one side or the other all the way to a spot known as Pompey's Pillar."[16]

Eliza's letters to James centered on life at Fort Rice and their son. When the news broke that the Seventh Cavalry would be returning from the expedition to their new post at Fort Abraham Lincoln, James was quick to let his wife know. Eliza and David were at the fort when Porter's assignment concluded.

"Fort Lincoln was built with quarters for six companies. The barracks for soldiers were on the side of the parade ground nearest the river, while seven detached houses for officers faced the river opposite," Elizabeth Custer wrote about the post in her book, *Boots and Saddles*.

Fort Lincoln in full view, 1875
COURTESY OF THE NATIONAL PARK SERVICE, LITTLE BIGHORN BATTLEFIELD NATIONAL MONUMENT,
LIBI-00019_00214, PHOTOGRAPHED BY AN UNKNOWN PHOTOGRAPHER, CIRCA 1875

The Porters occupied one of the homes designated for officers. Like all officers and their wives in Custer's command, Eliza and James enjoyed time with George and Elizabeth at dinner parties, picnics, and on fishing trips. When James was working, Eliza was a part of a reading club organized by Elizabeth and attended by Maggie Calhoun, Annie Yates, Nettie Smith, and Molly McIntosh.[17]

For the most part, the Porters' life at Fort Abraham Lincoln raising their son and spending time with a supportive group of friends was a happy one. When news reached the officers' wives that there were hostile Native Americans in close proximity of the post, Eliza began to worry about their future in the Dakota Territory.

In mid-February 1874, a troubling newspaper article from the *Boston Post* made the rounds at the fort. It reported that Custer had received word from the War Department that a "threatening raid of mounted Cheyenne and Sioux could not be resisted because there were no horseshoes in the Quartermaster's Department." James did his best to assure Eliza the Seventh Cavalry was "capable and ready to defend the post and the residents who lived there," but she was still concerned that the number of warring Native Americans might grow and become too overwhelming.[18]

By July 1874, the Porters were separated again. This time the lieutenant traveled with Custer on the Black Hills Expedition. Eliza said good-bye to her husband and the other members of the Seventh Cavalry on July 2. She didn't expect to see him again until the fall, and she worried for his safety. Various Sioux tribes under Sitting Bull were opposed to the army's plans to build another post. Rumor had it that they would strongly resist any attempt by the Seventh Cavalry to follow orders.[19]

An Indian missionary had visited Fort Abraham Lincoln in mid-July, bringing news that the Indians intended to contest every foot of the march. He begged General Custer to give up the expedition to prevent bloodshed. When Eliza learned about the warning, she, too, believed the expedition should be abandoned. James informed his wife that the treaty with the Sioux gave the United States the right to pass through and explore all the contested territory and that the Seventh Cavalry was prepared to face whatever happened as a result. Eliza didn't put up a fight but shared with her husband her belief that the expedition would lead to a severe conflict with the Indians.[20]

Although Eliza had never accompanied her husband on field expeditions as Elizabeth had with Custer, she felt the same as Elizabeth about being away from her husband. "Whatever peril might be awaiting me on the expedition, nothing could be equal to the suffering of suspense at home," Elizabeth wrote in her memoirs.[21]

Scouts carrying letters routinely traveled back and forth from where the Seventh Cavalry was located on the trek from Fort Abraham Lincoln. Eliza and James corresponded regularly, always professing their undying love for one another and making plans for the future, which included more children. Both wanted a little girl that James wrote "should be as beautiful as her mother." In between writing letters—and waiting for them—Eliza joined Elizabeth and the other officers' wives at the Custers' quarters where they read aloud passages from various books to one another and played croquet.[22]

Custer's Black Hills Expedition ended with all the troops returning safely to Fort Abraham Lincoln on August 30, 1874. James was almost unrecognizable to Eliza. He was sunburned, his clothes were in disarray, and he had a thick beard. All the soldiers had a similar appearance, but, after a long bath and a shave, First Lieutenant Porter was just as he had been.[23]

By mid-September, a handful of companies were being dispatched from the fort to Louisiana to assist law enforcement in dealing with the Ku Klux Klan. Lieutenant Porter had experience standing up to the Klan and expected Company I, which he commanded, to be transferred to the Southeast. At that time, Eliza didn't want to leave the Dakota Territory and was relieved to learn James and his men were to remain at Fort Abraham Lincoln for a while longer.[24]

With the exception of a few issues that arose with the Unepapa band of Sioux Indians—they were upset over the arrest of their chief for the murder of veterinarian Dr. John Honsinger, who was part of the Yellowstone Expedition—life at Fort Abraham Lincoln between December 1874 and March 1875 was without major incident.

In April, there was talk that Custer would lead the Seventh Cavalry on another trek through the Black Hills. The expedition would not only explore the possibility of gold in the region but also serve as a show of force against the Sioux threatening to leave the Standing Rock Reservation. Eliza was heartsick over the idea that James would be leaving again.

The following month, the government decided against another expedition. Eliza was relieved, but the difficulties between the United States and the Sioux continued to fester. By June, news that a war party had left Standing Rock and was threatening to attack Fort Abraham Lincoln was widespread. The Sioux didn't attack the post, but they did take some of the army's livestock grazing nearby.[25]

On August 15, 1875, Eliza informed her husband she was going to have a baby. Their second child was to be born in March of the following year. Now that the couple would be parents of two, Eliza hoped James would consider transferring to another unit. She wanted to return to South Carolina where the threat of being attacked by members of the Sioux Nation wasn't a possibility.

Days after the Porters found out they had another child on the way, Eliza read a special dispatch in a copy of the *Boston Globe* about a "pony dance" the Indians at Standing Rock had held. According to the article, this particular pony dance involved "riding into the quarters of the military commander of the reservation and trampling the tents and blankets of the officer and his troops." The report noted that the "Sioux and other tribes have assumed a threatening attitude and have vowed to drive all white settlers out of the territory."[26] The Indians were on the rampage, and Eliza was afraid for her family. On October 20, 1875, her fears were realized when warriors attacked Fort Abraham Lincoln.

Hostile camps advanced toward the post from the southwest and divided into war parties of forty or fifty warriors. The Indians' intent was to attack, but Arikara scouts for the US Army thwarted their attempts. Two companies of mounted recruits were reportedly en route from Kansas to bolster the Seventh Cavalry's defense. Those soldiers chased the party of Sioux to the Little Heart River, and from there "the warriors scattered, leaving no trail."[27]

The Porters welcomed their second son into the world on March 25, 1876, and named him James Francis. The situation between the military, the Sioux, and other tribes continued to escalate, and the likelihood the Seventh Cavalry would be sent to restore order at Standing Rock grew. At Eliza's insistence, James submitted a formal request to be made a part of the general staff through the proper chain of command. The general staff in the military was a group of officers that "assisted the commander of a division or larger unit by formulating and disseminating his policies, transmitting his orders, and overseeing their execution." The hope with the move was that James's involvement in any battle would be limited.[28]

On May 17, 1876, General Custer and his officers, including Lieutenant Porter, departed Fort Lincoln on the Bighorn Expedition. The purpose of the expedition, according to the June 1, 1876, edition of the *Leavenworth Times*, "was to punish the hostile Sioux." The Seventh Cavalry's objective was to find the "bands of Native Americans that have scattered themselves into the mountains, slaying the white invaders of their reservation, and return them to the areas [in which] they are to be confined."[29]

Just before marching off with the other soldiers, Lieutenant Porter bid good-bye to his family. His four-year-old son David clung to his father's leg, and Eliza hugged James's neck with their two-month-old baby cradled in his arms. "I fought the tears," she remarked in a note she later wrote to Elizabeth Custer. "I was crushed by his leaving and wanted to prolong that moment as long as he would allow."[30]

The battlefield in Montana where General Custer dismounted and fired on the advancing Sioux Indians; taken in 1886, these Seventh Cavalry soldiers are reenacting the scene.
COURTESY OF THE DENVER PUBLIC LIBRARY, SPECIAL COLLECTIONS

Drawing of the knoll where General George Custer and his men fell
COURTESY OF THE LIBRARY OF CONGRESS, LC-DIG-PPMSCA-22608

On June 27, 1876, the remains of the slain members of the Seventh Cavalry were identified and buried where they fell. Major Marcus Reno and fellow officers, positioned on high ground above the Little Bighorn River during the fight, noted in their account of the happenings that they saw three Seventh Cavalry prisoners tied to stakes in the Indian village on the other side of the water's edge. They speculated that one of those three men was Lieutenant James Porter. The captives were reportedly cut to pieces with axes and hatchets and their remains burned in bonfires until nothing remained but ashes and pieces of bone.[31]

Eliza and her sons remained in Strong, Maine, for a time after the memorial service for her husband. On September 18, 1876, she wrote a letter to Elizabeth Custer to let her know how she and her children were getting along.[32]

My Dear Mrs. Custer,

I regret so much that I could not have seen you the day you left Fort Lincoln, but of course, you knew that it was because I did not have a moment to leave the house. I was nearly wild with preparations for my tedious journey. But I have thought since that heartache it was best that I did not yet [have] time to see you, for in the state of mind I was in I would have done nothing but wept.

I dream often of those who have so nobly died. I will have an album on the lives done for them. Do you know when you can get Lieutenant Reiley's [sic] information to me?* I don't know his people or where they are.

I am very comfortably situated at my father-in-law's home occupying the room that we will need always. When we came home together there were many lonely nights. There are many lonely times before me this coming winter, and my heart aches when I realize what has happened. But all one can do is look forward to the time we shall meet on that beautiful shore by and by. What a happy moment that will be.

---

* Second Lieutenant William V. W. Reily was a friend of the Porters who had transferred to the Seventh Cavalry on January 25, 1876. He died with Custer on Last Stand Hill.

Last Sunday we had James's memorial service. The church was trimmed with mourning bunting and a profusion of flowers with Janice and Chrysanthemum plants draped around. It looked pretty. It was a hard day for me. The church was crowded. My sister went with me. Oh, how desolate everything looks to me. It seems at times that I could never rise up again. And then, I try to look up and think of my poor children. For them I must be wisely ordained to direct my thoughts.

I wish you would write me. I feel that we best understand how the other feels. If not for my children, I could not endure life long. My baby grows and is so cunning. He has seven teeth and is not yet six months old.

I heard from Mrs. Godfrey last night.* They are enjoying their lives; I would judge by her letter.

I'd like to ask you for a picture of the General, one of the unfortunate. I am making one of my own darling and will exchange with you. Many are very good indeed. . . .

Remember me with much love to your niece, Emma Reed, and also to Mrs. Calhoun. Am going to write her to send with this. I hope to hear that you are gaining strength fast. Can you give me Mrs. McIntosh's address? I would like to write her soon.

Bear up. Bear on. The end shall tell. Our dear Lord beareth all things well.

Sincerely yours,

Mrs. Porter[33]

Three months after Eliza sent her letter to Elizabeth, her son James became ill. He died on December 9, 1876, and was laid to rest beside his father's grave marker.[34]

---

* Mary Godfrey is the Mrs. Godfrey referred to. Her husband, Lieutenant Edward S. Godfrey, was a survivor of the Battle of the Little Bighorn.

CHAPTER SEVEN

Dreadful Darkness

SEVEN SEVENTH CAVALRY OFFICERS' WIVES BECAME WIDOWS ON JUNE 25, 1876. Six of those ladies lived out the rest of their years in constant communication with one another. They visited each other in their homes and traveled together to various tributes for their husbands. In person and in letters, the widows discussed the difficulties of carrying on without their spouses, the financial hardships they were facing, and how best to handle the public criticism of the Seventh Cavalry and General Custer. The bond the women shared proved to be what they needed to survive. Each admitted to family or in their memoirs the crucial necessity of their friendships.

Grace Harrington, wife of Lieutenant Henry Moore Harrington, chose not to stay in close touch with the other widows. Unlike Elizabeth Custer, Annie Yates, Maggie Calhoun, Molly McIntosh, Nettie Smith, and Eliza Porter, the remains of Grace's husband could not be found nor could any personal effects be identified that indicated where he last was on

Lieutenant Henry Harrington
CLASS ALBUM COLLECTION, US MILITARY ACADEMY LIBRARY

the battlefield. There was no information at all regarding his whereabouts or if he had survived the savage fight. He was listed as missing in action.[1] It was a declaration Grace couldn't accept.

According to a letter written to Elizabeth Custer from Nettie Smith in December 1876, "Mrs. Harrington is adrift with no resolve. She has kindly declined any effort to be consoled. As her husband is the only one of the soldiers missing without a trace, she believes there is a chance he lived through the ordeal and must be rescued."[2]

An article from the July 7, 1876, edition of the *Inter Ocean* listing the history of the deceased troops noted the likelihood Lieutenant Harrington was alive was extremely remote. "[O]f course, there is a bare possibility that this officer may have escaped," the article read, "but men of experience in the wars of the borders, when asked a question on the subject, shrug their shoulders and say he had better have been killed. The shrug and the remark suggest nameless horrors in connection with his name."[3]

Grace Berard and Henry Moore Harrington were married on November 15, 1872. Both were born in New York. Grace was born in August 1848 and Henry in April 1849. The Harringtons moved from New York to Michigan when Henry was a young boy, and he was raised in the town of Coldwater. After graduating from school, he attended the Cleveland Institute at University Heights in Ohio. He left the school in 1869 to help run his father's bakery. Prior to returning to Coldwater, he was invited to attend the Naval Academy, but declined their request. He preferred the army and, in time, was offered a congressional appointment to West Point. In Henry's last year at the military school, he met Grace Berard. She lived four miles away from West Point, in Highland Falls, New York.[4]

After graduating seventeenth in his class on June 14, 1872, Henry was made a second lieutenant and assigned to Company C of the Seventh Cavalry. He and Grace were first dispatched to Louisville, Kentucky, the headquarters for the Seventh Cavalry. From Kentucky, Henry was stationed in Charlotte, North Carolina. The Seventh Cavalry was scheduled to be sent to a Western outpost, and Henry was responsible

No image of Grace Harrington exists. This photograph is of Grace and Lieutenant Harrington's daughter, Grace Aileen Harrington. It's said the two favored one another a great deal.
COURTESY OF HARGRETT RARE BOOK & MANUSCRIPT LIBRARY / UNIVERSITY OF GEORGIA LIBRARIES

for training the troops. In addition to running the company through the standard drills, Henry and the others helped in the fight against the Ku Klux Klan. Several individuals associated with the racist organization were captured.[5]

The Harringtons' first child, Grace Aileen, was born during Henry and Grace's time in North Carolina.[6]

In February 1873, General Custer was ordered to unite the Seventh Cavalry, stationed at various posts, and lead them into the Dakota Territory. On March 2, 1873, Henry wrote a letter to his hometown newspaper in Coldwater about the future movement:[7]

[It's been a] few days since we received orders from the War Department to prepare to remove our troops from the Department of the South to the Department of the Dakota. Yesterday, an order came from our Regimental Headquarters in Louisville, Kentucky, warning

us to be ready to start on the receipt of a telegraphic order. We are all ready and may receive the order within a few minutes or may not for a week or two. So, it goes.

We will move by rail from here to Memphis and by steamer from there to Fort Randall, on the Missouri River near the southern boundary of Dakotah [sic]. This Fort will be the rendezvous of the Regiment for the present. From there our Companies will be scattered to the four winds. Some of us will be sent to the headwaters of the Missouri to act as scouts among the Indian tribes, and I shall be out all summer with a detachment as an escort of engineers on the Northern Pacific Railroad. May not have any fighting or may have a good deal, as the Sioux are in that part of the country. I wish I could get leave to visit you on the way, but it is impossible. I must be with my troop, as there is more to be attended to on such a trip than at any other time.[8]

The Seventh Cavalry and their wives were to report first to Fort Rice. Henry would proceed to the Dakota Territory with his company on horseback. Grace and their daughter would make their way to the post by train along with the other officers' wives. A winter snowstorm forced the train to stop near the town of Yankton. Grace and the baby took a room at the local hotel, but Henry and the rest of the Seventh Cavalry pitched canvas tents on the open prairie and tried to settle in while enduring frigid temperatures, high winds, and heavy snowdrifts.[9]

Henry wrote to Grace during his time away from her as well as the editor of the *Coldwater Republican* newspaper.[10]

Here I am at Yankton. Have been here since Saturday, the 12th [April], and just as busy as I could be. Since Sunday morning, we are having one of the hardest storms I ever saw. Two or three of the men are so badly frozen they will probably die. It is a severe change coming direct from North Carolina. Yesterday morning I marched on as officer of the guard and had to remain in camp, everything under snow. I remained there twenty-four hours with nothing to eat except one hard tack, which I dug out of the snow in one of the cooking tents.

This morning the officer of the day and myself started in. The only way we could find the hotel was by going a half a mile out of our way and striking the railroad and following the road. It is one of those hard snowstorms, snowing and blowing and covering everything about three feet under drifts. We had a pleasant and comfortable trip coming here, but this is rather a cool welcome to Dakota Territory. There are now ten cavalry companies here. We start on horseback across the country for Fort Rice, via Fort Randall, as soon as this snow melts and the grass starts. Letters for some days to come will reach me here.[11]

The Yankton residents were kind to the soldiers' wives, and Grace was charmed by the officers' spouses, particularly Elizabeth. She was attentive to Grace and the other women, but her time with them was limited. Elizabeth preferred to live with her husband in the field. If not for her baby, Grace would have chosen to be with Henry. He was scheduled to embark on the Yellowstone Expedition in June. The reason for the mission was the protection of the engineering parties of the Northern Pacific Railroad, who were making surveys for the location of the line between the Missouri River and the Rocky Mountains.[12]

When the Harringtons arrived at Fort Rice, they found the living quarters unfit for habitation. Henry decided his wife and child should travel to Coldwater to stay with his family. Grace and the baby would meet him at the fort once the expedition had concluded and the post was made ready for families to live there. Henry wrote letters about the expedition to his wife and also continued to communicate with the editor of the *Coldwater Republican*. One of his letters appeared in the July 26, 1873, edition of paper.[13]

We are now in camp about 175 miles northwest of Fort Rice, en route for the Yellowstone. The weather has been almost constantly stormy. Day before yesterday we marched 35 miles; were about 15 hours in marching from one camp to the other, but during the time were obliged to build a bridge 30 feet long over water, and 20 feet over swamp. I was ordered to build this bridge and did so out of the only material to be found, very crooked logs.

The Railroad Engineers left Fort Lincoln with a small escort a few days before we left Fort Rice. We joined them yesterday. This outfit is now to be divided into two parts. One half is to put on at once for the Yellowstone. The other is to remain with the engineers. The former, upon their arrival, will build a post to protect our supplies while we are still farther west.

I went out this forenoon after antelope; shot one. I was obliged to remain very near our column as we constantly see signs of Indians in our vicinity. I came in from my hunt just after they formed camp and found that within an hour's time an escort was to start back for Fort Lincoln with an ambulance containing a man with a broken leg. I am sorry for the man, but glad of this opportunity to send letters back to civilization. I am very well indeed, standing the trip first rate.

Affectionately Yours,

H. W. H.[14]

On August 16, 1873, the *Coldwater Republican* featured another letter from Henry about the wonders of the West.

The vast territory of the Northwest so long known as the Missouri and the Oregon Territories have been divided and subdivided, new names have been given, until even intelligent men need not blush if they are unable without study rightly to locate all the names with which modern geographies abound. Among these is the Wyoming Territory, situated about the headwaters of the Yellowstone. Like the far-famed vale of Wyoming in the west, long ago made famous by the poet's pen, so this, its western namesake, seems destined to win for itself renown on account of the wonders of its natural scenery.[15]

Here, lying partly in Wyoming and partly in Montana, lies the tract of country some fifty-five miles square which Congress has set apart forever as a National Park. This tract embraces the Fire Hole Basin, the Great Geysers, Yellowstone Lake, the Upper and Lower

Falls of the Yellowstone, the Great Canyon and numberless hot and boiling springs and volcanos. . . .

Here I am seated in my tent on the bank of the far-famed Yellowstone, writing on a book resting on my knee. We are about 225 miles from Fort Lincoln, encamped 15 miles below the mouth of [the] Powder River. Since writing last, we have been making all kinds of marches, from five to twenty miles each day, coming in a very round about course. We are to cross the river here and march about 150 miles farther and then return to [Fort] Lincoln over the same trail, there to winter. I suppose we are to go over the same thing next season. But I will not anticipate . . . For there is some evil even amid all that

On a number of occasions, Elizabeth would send for her friends to visit. This photograph was taken in 1874 and is of Tom Custer and another soldier transporting two of Elizabeth's friends to Fort Lincoln.
COURTESY OF THE NATIONAL PARK SERVICE, LITTLE BIGHORN BATTLEFIELD NATIONAL MONUMENT, LIBI-00019_00339, PHOTOGRAPHED BY AN UNKNOWN PHOTOGRAPHER, "THOMAS CUSTER, COLONEL WILLIAM W. COOKE, AND THE WADSWORTH GIRLS IN A SPRING WAGON BESIDE THE RIVER, CIRCA 1874"

Amateur theatrics were a means of entertainment for General Custer, Elizabeth, the Seventh Cavalry officers, and their wives during their time at Fort Lincoln. Here, General Custer and his sister, Margaret, pose as members of the Quaker Peace Commission.

COURTESY OF THE NATIONAL PARK SERVICE, LITTLE BIGHORN BATTLEFIELD NATIONAL MONUMENT, LIBI-00019_00290, PHOTOGRAPHED BY ORLANDO SCOTT GOFF, CIRCA 1875 *is novel and wonderful. Sleeping at night on a buffalo robe spread upon the ground, which a stealthy rattlesnake may crawl to share as your bed fellow; arising every morning at 3 o'clock, breakfasting and packing so as to start on the march at 5 o'clock, and going into camp at any time from 2 to 7 p.m., as the nature of the locality may prove.*

As yet we have had no trouble with Indians, but we are told a large number are awaiting us on the other side of the river where game is more abundant.[16]

Grace and the baby were waiting at Fort Abraham Lincoln to greet Henry when Custer and his command returned to the post. The Harringtons enjoyed their time together, and, when they weren't spending time playing with their daughter and taking long walks around the post, they could be found making visits to the Custers' quarters. Elizabeth and George hosted regular dinner parties and invited the officers and their wives to the soirees. Henry and Grace were present for a number of the special events at the fort, including the celebration of military promotions and weddings such as the one held in late summer 1874 between Lieutenant Francis Gibson and Katherine Garrett. After spending some time at the post, the pair traveled twenty-four miles south to Fort Rice where Henry would be stationed on a regular basis. Improvements had been completed at the fort, and it was now fit for women and children.[17]

On July 2, 1874, Grace and the other officers' wives were once again left alone as their husbands, along with the rest of the Seventh Cavalry, accompanied General Custer on the Black Hills Expedition. According to the July 4, 1874, edition of Chicago's *Inter Ocean* newspaper, it was anticipated that the soldiers would not return before October, once a thorough exploration of the legendary region had been completed and after they had established a site for the building of the fort and trading post. The article, eagerly read by Grace and the other wives, reported that it was probable "a strong resistance [would] be made by the Indians, as startling rumors are constantly arriving at this place of the gathering of the different Sioux tribes under Sitting Bull."[18]

Just as he had when he was part of the Yellowstone Expedition, Lieutenant Harrington wrote letters not only to Grace but also to the editor of the *Coldwater Republican* newspaper. His letter dated July 15, 1874, was written from a camp in Montana.[19]

Here we are, after a long, tedious march, laying over for one day in order to give our animals rest. Since leaving Fort Lincoln on the 2nd [of July], we have been constantly on the march, averaging 20 miles a day.

We expect that about 2½ days more will bring us to the point of our destination, the Black Hills. The country through which we have thus far marched is very broken. Once in a while we strike a fine valley, such as the one [in which] we are now encamped, which looks as if it would make a fine agricultural country; but generally, the land only produces cactus and sagebrush.

The Indians tell us the country of the Black Hills, which we are about to open up, is almost a paradise, with large forests, fine mountain streams, good land, abundance of game, and what most men care for, lots of gold. We shall soon see what there is of it.[20]

Grace was relieved when the cavalry returned earlier than expected from its tour. While certainly concerned for Henry's safety, she also wanted him to be home in time for the birth of their second child. Just before Henry made it back to Fort Rice, he penned another letter to his friends in New York to let them know if indeed gold had been discovered. The letter appeared in the September 19, 1874, edition of the *Coldwater Republican*. "If anyone asks what I say about gold in the Black Hills," Henry wrote, "tell them there is undoubtedly some there, but whether in large quantities or not is as yet impossible to say. A little was found in several different places. Perhaps more might have been found had we been able to spend more time in prospecting.[21]

"In one valley where we camped, they panned out considerable. The miners with us said it would not pay to pan, but they could sluice out about ten dollars a day. This was our richest find. So, tell those who ask what I say that if they get enough to eat at home they had better stay there; if no, they had better go almost anywhere else rather than to the Black Hills for some time to come."[22]

The Harringtons welcomed their son, Henry Berard, into the world on September 26, 1874. Life for the family was idyllic for a time. The lieutenant served as quartermaster with Custer's command at Fort Rice. He was responsible for making sure equipment, materials, and firearms were available and in working order, and for providing support for soldiers and units in the field. Harrington was home at nights with Grace and their children.

The growing tensions with the Native Americans living at the Standing Rock Reservation between Fort Rice and the Grand River were the source of many after-dinner conversations between the couple. The news that Washington was sending additional troops stationed in Louisiana to Fort Rice and Fort Abraham Lincoln worried Grace. Henry assured her that the Seventh Cavalry could defend both posts should any confrontation arise.[23]

In early May 1875, Lieutenant Harrington was granted a leave of absence from duty and decided he and Grace would take their children to see their grandparents. They were anxious to introduce their new son to their families. The Harringtons traveled first to Coldwater, Michigan. The May 29, 1875, edition of the *Coldwater Republican* reported on their stay and how the pair expected to be visiting relatives throughout the winter. By September 1875, Henry and Grace were on their way to Hillsdale, New York, to spend time with her kin.[24]

On March 6, 1876, Lieutenant Harrington received a dispatch from Custer informing him that the general and his command in the Black Hills were ordered to take the field, and that, if he desired to accompany them, he needed to report at once to Fort Abraham Lincoln. Henry packed his things, kissed his wife and children good-bye, and hurried to his assignment. Grace heard from her husband next in mid-April.[25]

"When we arrived at Fargo [Dakota Territory] we found that a storm had filled the cuts on the railroad west full, but that they were to start a train out Monday morning to open it," Henry wrote on April 11, 1876. "We took that train and have wished often since that we had not. We had two engines—one of them with a snowplow, 50 shovelers and 20 cars

The officers' quarters at Fort Rice behind the post cemetery, 1871
COURTESY OF THE STATE HISTORICAL SOCIETY OF NORTH DAKOTA, 00670-00052

loaded with fuel, boarding cars, etc. We managed to 'ditch' the engines and 'toot caboose' twice, delaying us nearly a day each time, and the snow was so full that it was slow work anyway.

"We finally arrived here about 7 p.m. last Friday evening, having been only 12 days making the distance from Fargo here, 100 miles. When we got here, the fuel was more than half gone, and there was none here. The train had to leave us here and start back to Fargo after more. They have found a good deal of snow drifted since they went over the road, and have not reached Fargo yet, but expect to arrive there tonight. We have to wait here till they fix up their engines, load up the fuel, and get back here. Don't know how long that will be. When they get here, we will start on, and there is so much snow in the cuts west of here that they expect to be about two weeks getting through."[26]

Grace was not certain how long Henry would be away on the latest expedition. He and the other members of the Seventh Cavalry had left Fort Abraham Lincoln for Montana on May 17, 1876. For a while, she was content to stay with her parents, but, by the end of May she decided to return to Fort Rice. She wanted to be at the post when Henry came home. She had no way of knowing then that Henry was never coming home.

Grace Harrington was among twenty-five women at Fort Rice who became widows on June 25, 1876. According to the July 26, 1876, edition of the *Fall River Daily Evening News*, the scene at the post when word reached officers there that Custer and his men had all been killed was "chaotic." When the wives, most with small children, were informed of the demise of their husbands, "utter grief and helplessness overcame them."[27]

Grace listened closely as the survivors of the Battle of the Little Bighorn who returned to Fort Rice gently answered the grieving widows' questions about how their husbands had died, and if their bodies had been buried or were being brought back to the post. Some were presented with buttons, letters, or other personal items found on or around their spouses' remains. The sorrowful women eagerly took the mementos, some crying as they held the items. There was nothing to be given to Grace.

In late July, Grace Harrington left Fort Rice with her children in tow. She was still in a state of shock when she arrived at her parents' home in Highland Falls, New York. Grace's in-laws had been informed of Henry's death on July 10, 1876. The report had come from the military and not their daughter-in-law. She was unable to process the loss or admit that Henry was gone. Lieutenant Harrington's parents held a memorial service for their son on August 20, 1876. A headstone was placed at the Coldwater Cemetery in his memory.[28]

For several months, Grace was inconsolable. She often refused to leave her room. In a letter dated January 12, 1877, written by Grace's brother, Robert, to Elizabeth Custer, the family was "quite concerned about her condition." They consulted with a local physician who informed them Grace was suffering from "extreme melancholy." The doctor called her affliction "a kind of delirium." A specialized diet and a regimen of rest and relaxation was prescribed. "The children are well cared for by all our family," Robert shared with Elizabeth. "We are hopeful that in due time our dear Grace will recover."[29]

By late March, Grace had improved and had assumed much of the responsibility of caring for her son and daughter. In reviewing her finances, it suddenly became important for her to find work. Her sole source of income was a $15 a month pension from the army. Robert, an employee with Tiffany and Company, along with a few influential

Highland Falls residents, wrote President Grant for assistance for the grieving widow. He responded by appointing her postmistress of Highland Falls Village, New York.

Grant's decision was a controversial one. Mr. J. Nelson, the postmaster whom Grace was to be replacing, was unhappy with the president's appointment. Nelson had held the position for more than sixteen years and did not want to give up the job.[30] According to an article in the May 15, 1877, edition of the *Evening Gazette*, he had earned a substantial amount of money as postmaster. Grant's plan to reform such civil service postings was to limit the term to no more than eight years. Nelson had been there too long in the president's estimation.[31]

After Grant left office in March 1877, Nelson contested Grace's appointment, and it was canceled before the commission was issued. She was still emotionally fragile when the incident was reported in newspapers from New York to Louisiana. "Mrs. Grace Harrington, wife of the late Lieutenant H. M. Harrington, of the Seventh Cavalry, who was killed with Custer at the Battle of the Little Bighorn, was appointed postmistress at Highland Falls about a month ago," an article in the *New Orleans Republican* noted. "She got her bond approved and has been waiting all this time for her commission, which has not come, but instead a man of considerable wealth and influence was appointed in her place. Mrs. Harrington's friends are indignant because the office is worth only about $400 a year, that it should be given to a man of property, while she is compelled to support herself and several children on a pension of $18 a month."[*][32]

Disappointed that the chance to be postmistress had passed her by, Grace tabled the idea of finding employment. Instead, she became preoccupied with the idea that Lieutenant Harrington was alive and being held captive somewhere. She dreamed she saw her husband's face and heard his voice calling out to her for help. "My dear Mrs. Custer," she wrote Elizabeth in February 1878, "How can I entertain the thought of pressing on when my Henry is waiting for me to find him?"[33]

While the other widowed ones were rebuilding their lives, Grace Harrington was trapped in a thick and dreadful darkness—unable to move forward and begin to quiet her grief.

---

[*] The newspaper report was incorrect. Grace had only two children, and her pension was just $15 a month.

Chapter Eight

Alone in the Shadows

The town of Monroe, Michigan, was blanketed in snow on the morning of December 25, 1876. The yard in front of the Custers' home and the street beyond resembled an unfinished painting. Much of the canvas was perfectly white, waiting for an artist's hand to bring color into the scene.

Elizabeth sat by the window in her room watching the morning light struggle through the fog and cold. At some point, she would need to get dressed and join her in-laws for breakfast, but she lacked the will to move. It was her first Christmas without her husband, and the near paralyzing grief she thought she had learned to control had found her again.

As Elizabeth turned away from the window, her eyes settled on a framed photograph of Custer sitting on her bureau. She remembered the awful moment when she had first heard the news of his death. She would never forget the devastated look on the faces of the wives who had also lost their husbands that day. "From that time the life went out of the hearts of the women who wept," Elizabeth wrote in her memoirs, "and God asked them to walk alone in the shadows."[1]

In the six months Custer had been gone, condolences had poured in from sincere citizens across the country. Many came from civilians who knew of General Custer's reputation and of his accomplishments in the Civil War; some came from politicians who had met the couple during one of their visits to Washington; and some were written by men who had been a part of the expeditions to Yellowstone or the Black Hills.

Elizabeth and General Custer relaxing in their headquarters at Fort Lincoln, 1875
COURTESY OF THE NATIONAL PARK SERVICE, LITTLE BIGHORN BATTLEFIELD NATIONAL MONUMENT,
LIBI_00019_00219, PHOTOGRAPHED BY ORLANDO SCOTT GOFF

Brevet Lieutenant Colonel Jacob Lyman Greene wrote Elizabeth on July 15, 1876, to express his sorrow over her loss. Greene served as Custer's best man at their wedding and was also his assistant adjutant general during the Civil War. "Since the news of your husband's death I am continually going over the scenes of our service together," the officer wrote. "I well remember how I was perpetually dreading his death, and that it seemed to me I could never serve with another officer. And as he went into one danger after another and came out unharmed, and almost my first fight with him at Culpepper after which we went home together, I began to feel that the man bore a charmed life. . . .

"I never loved and admired any other man as I did your husband. What he was to you and what you were to him I well know. You were the first and only love of one of the bravest, strongest and noblest of men, whose mark in the history of this country and of his profession will never be lost, and whose death was the seal of a record, the most brilliant in deeds and without a stain of dishonor."[2]

In addition to letters from those strongly associated with Custer was correspondence from Elizabeth's cousin, Rebecca Richmond. Rebecca was the niece of Elizabeth's father, and the two were close friends. They confided in one another, and Rebecca's letters were a great source of comfort to the widow, like this one, dated December 4, 1876, from her home in Topeka, Kansas:[3]

Your sad letter, Libbie dear, came yesterday, and was very welcome, for it accorded with my feelings, it being the anniversary of the death of our precious Helen [a friend of the family]. . . .

But Libbie dear, let me assure you that I never have a sad day but what my heart goes out to you, for you are never absent from my thoughts, knowing your sorrows are so much harder than mine. . . .

I was sorry indeed to hear of the dear Mrs. Custer's [Elizabeth's mother-in-law] suffering and serious illness. No doubt brought on by such loss. After so many years of suffering both mental [sic] and physical [sic], it seems sad to know that an old person's last days should be filled with such pain. Do give her my best, please, Libbie, and tell her how glad I am that I know her and how sorry I am that she is ill. I wish there were some way to relieve her pain.

These holiday times are indeed sad days. For you, I hope you will have strength to endure your trials. They really seem too great for one to bear. You know, Libbie, I can't comfort you, I can only grieve with you and commend you, as I do twice daily, to our Heavenly Father.[4]

Among the letters that offered comfort and concern were insensitive requests for articles of Custer's clothing and letters he had written over his lifetime. On December 13, 1876, Charles Buxton, with the stock brokerage firm Camblos and Myers, wrote Elizabeth asking her to send "your husband's autograph and a swatch from one of his uniforms." Buxton enclosed a stamped envelope for the widow's convenience.[5]

Several letters sent to Elizabeth made no mention of her husband's death at all. The authors of the letters had questions and wanted Elizabeth to give them answers. People wanted to know what kind of man General Custer was; what he thought of his superior officers; and what had really happened at the Battle of the Little Bighorn.

Elizabeth had been pondering some of those questions herself. Military leaders were blaming Custer for the massacre, claiming he had disobeyed orders. General Terry formally reported that Custer did not wait for another column of troops to arrive before pressing ahead to meet the Indians. With few exceptions, Custer's most ardent critics cited his arrogance and independent thinking for the unnecessary loss of lives. Major Marcus Reno, one of the commanders of a battalion of the Seventh Cavalry present at the Battle of the Little Bighorn, told his superiors that among the many mistakes Custer had made was not taking Gatling guns with him when he left Fort Abraham Lincoln. Captain Fred Benteen, another of the commanders of one of the Seventh's battalions at the Little Bighorn, referred to Custer's tactics on the battlefield as "senseless valley hunting ad infinitum."[6]

Elizabeth was outraged by the accusation that Custer had been derelict in his duty. She defended his leadership skills and praised him as a hero. Among those who championed Custer's actions were General George McClellan, whom Custer served under during the Civil War; future commander of the Seventh Cavalry, Colonel James Forsyth; and fellow Seventh Cavalry officer, Captain Thomas Weir.[7]

Elizabeth received letters from all three supporters. McClellan reminded her that the same men who were now proclaiming that Custer had acted rashly would have also said he acted timidly if the Indians had escaped. Colonel Forsyth noted that George had followed the orders he'd been given and that he himself would not have done less.[8] Thomas's letter was heartbreaking and mysterious. He implied that Reno and Benteen had allowed Custer and his company to be killed. "I know if we were all of us alone in the parlor, at night, the curtains all drawn and everybody else asleep, one or the other would make me tell you everything," he wrote to Elizabeth. "If I can get away I am going to Monroe. I know I could say something to you all that would make you feel glad for a little while at least."[9]

Elizabeth thumbed through telegrams and notes in a pile next to Custer's picture. At the top of the stack was a card from Nettie Smith that featured an arrangement of white amaryllis and the sentiment which read: "Bright as a flower thy Christmas be." When Elizabeth later responded to Nettie, she thanked her for her thoughtfulness and shared with her that her Christmas morning had been filled with memories both good and bad. She recalled how heartbroken she had been when she

Elizabeth Custer a year before her husband's death

returned home after the memorial service in August 1876. She dreaded the tasks ahead of her. Elizabeth wrote in a note to Nettie how "daunting and dreary the thought of moving forward without Autie" was to her.[10]

One of the first things Elizabeth made herself do was go through Custer's personal belongings. The trunk he had carried with him from post to post, his uniforms, and his private notes and correspondence needed to be sorted through and organized. Before she began the difficult job, she reread a letter Rebecca Richmond had sent to her shortly after Custer was killed. The letter was comforting to Elizabeth and gave her strength to face the forlorn days ahead. "Your life with Armstrong has been intense, concentrated, three or four, or a dozen ordinary lives in one," Rebecca had written on August 11, 1876, "and those who can live over again quietly, thoughtfully, and I will say pleasurably, be near you. Libbie, how much rather would you be the early widow of such a man than the lifelong wife of many others!"[11]

Elizabeth painstakingly removed Custer's belongings from his leather footlocker and placed them reverently beside her on the floor. Two of the items were passes for travel on the Northern Pacific Railroad. One of the tickets was made out to General Custer and the other to Elizabeth. Among the newspaper clippings, animal hides, photographs, and tickets were letters from colleagues and relatives. Elizabeth casually leafed through thank-you notes, bulletins, and dispatches until she came across a love letter written in a hand she didn't recognize. "Dear General," the correspondence began, "Try and come down tonight if possible, for I have many things to say to you. Remember for I love you forever. Oh, do not disappoint me. For the love of heaven burn this as soon as you read it and oblige your own loving Nellie."[12]

Elizabeth speculated that the author of the love letter was Nellie Wadsworth. Nellie and her sister Emma had spent time at the Custers' home at Fort Abraham Lincoln. Custer had brought the ladies with him to the post after visiting Monroe in 1875. Before returning the letter to Custer's footlocker, Elizabeth jotted the woman's name down on the back of the letter. She knew that it wasn't unusual for her husband to have had admirers, and, of all the Nellies she and Custer had known, Nellie Wadsworth seemed the most likely candidate to have been involved with Custer.[13]

Elizabeth found other items of significant interest among Custer's things, including a life insurance policy worth $4,750 and an unpaid promissory note for $13,000. Knowing Custer as she did, the possibility that there were other unpaid debts was highly likely. Elizabeth pondered her bleak financial situation. She had been awarded $900 from a widows' fund created by the *New York Herald* newspaper; $197 from the United States Treasury for George's participation in the Belknap trial; and $500 from Grand Duke Alexis as a token of sympathy.*[14] After settling outstanding debts, helping support her elderly in-laws, and paying her moving expenses, Elizabeth had little left to pay for her own food, clothing, and shelter.

Knowing there were few jobs that respectable women could pursue added to Elizabeth's anxiety. Coming to terms with the fact that Custer was gone and dealing at last with the very real possibility he had been unfaithful with more than one woman, including a family friend, made the process of moving on with life almost unbearable. On a scrap of onionskin paper, Elizabeth jotted down what she believed was the only way she could get through the difficulties ahead and maintain her husband's reputation. In French she wrote, *Oublier! Oublier! C'est le secret de la vie.* ("To forget! To forget! It is the secret to life.")[15]

Prior to Thanksgiving 1876, Elizabeth reached the conclusion she would have to leave Monroe and move to a location where the job opportunities for women weren't so limited. Associates of Custer's at the US Pension Agency in Washington, DC, offered to help Elizabeth find work somewhere within the government, and suggested the possibility of a position with the post office. When President Grant was approached to facilitate an appointment for Elizabeth as postmistress of Monroe, he was enthusiastic about the idea. The Widow Custer explained that she would be in favor of such an appointment only if President Grant had nothing to do with helping her get the job. The president's public condemnation of General Custer's actions at the Battle of the Little Bighorn infuriated Elizabeth, and she wanted nothing to do with him or his administration.[16]

---

* The Belknap trial involved corruption at a trading post, and the Grand Duke Alexis was a Russian military leader who traveled to the United States in the early 1870s.

Elizabeth had friends living in New Jersey who invited her to travel to the state and investigate the jobs available there, and in New York. She made the move to the East Coast in early May 1877. Elizabeth immediately set out to find herself gainful employment and decided she would write about her marriage to Custer and defend his honor, which, in her estimation, had been "woefully maligned." President Grant had claimed Custer's military tactics were faulty and that he had willfully disobeyed orders. Custer had sent Elizabeth a copy of the orders he had been given, and she knew he had acted accordingly. "It is, of course, impossible to give you any definitive instructions," General Terry wrote to Custer prior to engaging the Indians in battle. "The Department Commander places too much confidence in your zeal, energy, and ability," Terry added, "to impress precise orders which might hamper your actions when nearly in contact with the enemy."[17]

Convinced her husband had been in the right, Elizabeth set about to stop the speculation and to defend his honor. She pushed for military leaders and politicians to stop talking about launching an inquiry into the happenings at the Little Bighorn and begin the much-needed hearings. Elizabeth also helped to organize fund-raising events and worked with committee chair members dedicated to building a monument in Custer's honor.[18]

Among those who had been vying for a chance to produce a bronze monument of Custer was sculptor George E. Bissell. Reverend H. Loomis of Poughkeepsie, New York, began writing Elizabeth in September 1876 to promote Bissell and his work. Loomis's letter provided the widow with a detailed and romantic description of the work he wanted to produce.

"Mrs. General Custer, Dear Madam, I am anxious to know if any plans are being made on securing a monument to the memory of General Custer," Reverend Loomis wrote. "Incredibly, on hearing of his death, I without hasting contacted a gifted sculptor, Mr. Bissell—the young sculptor of this place conceived the idea of making a model for an equestrian statue of the brave General. Much like the amazing leader, this tribute would be unique and glorious," the reverend remarked.[19]

While doing all she could to preserve her husband's good name, Elizabeth remained busy trying to find suitable employment. In early May 1877, she heard from Louisa Lee Schuyler, founder of the first nursing school in the United States. Elizabeth had written the woman known as the "Florence Nightingale of America" regarding job possibilities.[20] Schuyler replied in a letter dated April 13, 1877:

> *My dear Mrs. Custer,*
> *I have delayed in answering your letter of April 3rd until I could make a few inquiries in regard to charitable work in New York.*
> *Yesterday I saw Mrs. Osborne, one of the saints of this earth, a lady who has suffered her own bereavement (the loss of her two children) most nobly and who is always working for others. Mrs. Osborne is one of the supporters of our Training School for Nurses, a graduate of the New York State Charities Aid Association. I told her about you because I knew she would sympathize with you most truly.*
> *She asked me to send you the enclosed report and to say that should you care to apply to the school, she would arrange to have you admitted as soon as you may wish. Of course, I could not tell her whether you had any aptitude for hospital work. She suggested that should you care to consider the proposition at all, you might possibly come to Poughkeepsie and visit the hospital and learn from the ladies all about it. You could then decide better if you would like it.*
> *Your desire to enter the work force is commendable. I know you will persevere. Whoever has the humanity at heart cannot fail.*
> *Best Regards.[21]*

While Elizabeth was adjusting to life in New York, Emanuel and Maria Custer were struggling to adjust to being apart from her. A letter Emanuel penned to his daughter-in-law on June 10, 1877, expressed how much Elizabeth was missed.[22]

> *Well, Libbie, my dear and darling,*
> *Your letter of the 4th came duly to home on Friday, and I should have answered it yesterday if it had not been for sickness in the family.*

Elizabeth Custer's father-in-law,
Emanuel Custer
COURTESY OF THE MONROE COUNTY
MUSEUM SYSTEM, MONROE, MICHIGAN

Nettie has been sick all week, and I was afraid that she was going to die. But I am glad to say that she is much better today. I think she is entirely out of danger, and I feel glad that I can give an honorable report so you can see that I have had a very busy week.

Well, now my daughter, I was so glad to get your kind letter. I did begin to think that you had forgotten me. I want you to know that I remember you every day. I miss you very much, and I would like you to be with us all the time. You know how much I loved my dear Autie, and I know how much he loved you, and I can't help but love you as if you were my own dear child. . . .

Please don't stay away from home for too long. I should very much like to visit West Point if the remains of my dear and darling son should be brought there. I am going to think the time very long until you come home. You are all that is left of my dear Autie. . . .

My daughter, when you read this litter [sic] if you can read it because I struggle to write . . . I want you to burn it because if anyone should see it, they would say that it was some weak mind that wroat [sic] it. I have wroat [sic] just as I feel.

I remain your affectionate father,

E. Custer[23]

In July 1876, the wives of the officers who lost their lives at the Battle of the Little Bighorn began issuing requests to the army to have their husbands' bodies removed from the hasty plots where they had been placed and returned to them to receive proper burials. The widows were slow to receive a response. The project would be costly, and the military was in no hurry to approve the expensive venture.

In early March 1877, Elizabeth Custer decided to solicit help from one of General Custer's longtime friends, Colonel Michael Sheridan. The colonel's brother was Lieutenant General Phil Sheridan. He appealed to his brother to write General William Tecumseh Sherman to intercede on the widows' behalf, and the general agreed.[24]

> *The wives and friends of the officers who were killed with Custer . . . are pressing me to bring their bodies, and I wrote to ask if the Secretary of War will authorize the necessary expense. It is possible that there may be sufficient incidental funds in the Adjutant General's office, or other funds at the command of the Secretary, which can be used for this purpose. The sum required will be small.*
>
> *I propose in case it meets with the approbation of the Secretary, and yourself, to bury all the bodies, except General Custer, at Fort Leavenworth. Mrs. Custer wants General Custer buried at West Point, and I recommend that she be gratified in this desire.*
>
> *I can detail an officer to bring the bodies down in suitable boxes to Fort Lincoln and there transfer them to the proper coffins. The satisfaction it will give to the wives, families, and friends of the officers will be very great.*
>
> *I am, General, Yours truly,*
> *P. H. Sheridan*[25]

Permission for the army to exhume the bodies was granted in late April 1877. "I now have the honor to inform you that upon a reconsideration of the subject the Secretary of War has decided to pay, from the contingent funds of the army, for the expenses of bringing in the bodies of General Custer and the officers who fell with him," the adjutants' office informed Lieutenant General Phil Sheridan in a letter dated April 28, 1877.

A month later, Sheridan directed his brother, Lieutenant Michael Sheridan, to retrieve the bodies.[26]

The bodies of eleven officers and two civilians were exhumed and shipped to the homes of relatives for burial. Custer's remains arrived late in the summer of 1877 when the US Military Academy was not in session. A full-blown ceremony could not be marshaled at that time, and the funeral was postponed until the fall. Meanwhile, Custer's coffin was temporarily placed in a vault owned by a friend in Poughkeepsie, New York.[27]

Reverend Custer attended his son's funeral at West Point along with his beloved daughter-in-law on October 10, 1877. According to the October 11, 1877, edition of the *Brooklyn Daily Eagle*, the general's service was of a "most imposing character." Custer's body was taken from Poughkeepsie on the steamer *Mary Powell*, and cadets from the Poughkeepsie Military Institute, the mayor, city council members, and numerous citizens took part in the procession.[28]

The hearse was drawn by four black horses, and was decorated with flags and black crepe. The coffin containing the remains was draped with a flag, a single floral offering a shoulder strap with two stars formed of geraniums and immortelles. The stars were made of tuberoses. The horse with an empty saddle, which had all the equipment belonging to Custer's rank, followed the hearse. The remains were put ashore at West Point at twelve o'clock, under escort of the Poughkeepsie military.[29]

A detachment cavalry, under command of Brevet-Colonel Beaumont, received them, and with other escorts attended them to the chapel where they were deposited and left under guard. The hat and sword of General Custer was placed upon the coffin before the final service. Mrs. Custer was present at the services, attended by Major General Schofield. E. H. Custer, the father of General Custer, Mrs. Nettie Smith, his sister, and several other immediate relatives were present; also, Lieutenant Braden, of the Seventh Cavalry, who fought under Custer and had been several times wounded.

After the services, which consisted of the reading of a portion of the Episcopal burial service, with responses sung by a choir of cadets, the line of march was formed, and the procession moved to the cemetery.[30]

THE LAST HONORS OVER THE GRAVE.

FUNERAL OF GENERAL CUSTER.

General George Custer's funeral at West Point

Elizabeth received numerous letters from friends and acquaintances after Custer's funeral. One of those letters came from her childhood friend and frequent visitor to Fort Abraham Lincoln while the Custers lived there, Agnes Bates Wellington. "I'm thankful that this long experience is over for you, but I know full well that the agony of last June and of all the year between seems condensed into these few days," Agnes wrote the widow on July 31, 1877. "Even to me, it makes it all seem new and more heartbreaking than ever and more real. While they lay out there, I could not realize but that they were coming home again, but this last homecoming makes their deaths a reality."[31]

Angeline Augusta Cooke, mother of Lieutenant William Winer Cooke, who also died at the Little Bighorn, penned a sympathy letter to Elizabeth on October 13, 1877. "What a blessing it is to have received our loved ones at long last," the grieving mother wrote. "You will find it will soften the sorrow a very little to have our dear ones from that bleak, barren place."[32]

Elizabeth was grateful for the letters of compassion and support sent to her, but, for true understanding, she turned to the handful of women who had lived through the experience with her. Maggie Calhoun and Annie Yates traveled to New York to visit Elizabeth, and they were joined often by Nettie Smith. Grace Harrington and Molly McIntosh would commiserate with the widows through cards and telegrams. In the confines of the widows' circle, a term Elizabeth used to refer to the group, the women were able to express their true feelings. The widows had a set of beliefs they dedicated themselves to that guided their actions. Elizabeth jotted the motto down on a scrap of paper while staying at the Hotel Grenoble in New York in 1904. "Once a widow, always cautious. So difficult for a widow to preserve her reputation and enjoy the fleeting hours. Reputation is the result of caution. The paragraph of today wraps up the parcel of tomorrow. Everything but my stockings."[33]

The widows, particularly Elizabeth, knew the public was watching them and judging their every action. All took a vow not to remarry—not only because they worried what others would think, but because they believed the memories of their departed spouses would loom large over any other union. "I'm not in favor of second marriages for women, as a general thing," Annie Yates wrote Elizabeth on August 5, 1877. "The only thing that makes them at all proper in my eyes is love as pure, as deep, and sincere as the woman ever gave before." Elizabeth felt as Annie did. At thirty-four she knew she would never love again and would dedicate her life to Custer's legacy.[34]

After searching for several months, Elizabeth secured a part-time position with the New York Sanitary Commission, a government agency that raised money for veterans and their widows, and ran kitchens in army camps, soldiers' homes, and homes for disabled veterans. Elizabeth's job entailed maintaining the incoming and outgoing letters for the organization and helping to collect donations.[35]

Elizabeth used any spare moment she had to write books about her life in the army with Custer, and her memoirs, *Boots and Saddles, Following the Guidon,* and *Tenting on the Plains,* sold well. In a conversation with a *Rochester Herald* newspaper reporter, Elizabeth admitted that the popularity of her first book, *Boots and Saddles,* came as a surprise. "It dealt with only three years of life on the frontier and gave but a small part of General Custer's history," the article read. "My next work will be larger and will cover a period extending over nineteen years. It will be a concise account of General Custer's career on the frontier. I was with him much of the time, and the book will be written in a narrative form largely . . .[36]

"I have not begun the book, and it will be a work of time as I must depend largely upon memory for my facts. I never kept a diary during our life in the West as I never supposed an occasion would arise to use it. There is a mass of information regarding the General which will be given to the public in this book for the first time."[37]

By 1892, Elizabeth had become financially self-sufficient and used her income to build a home for herself in Bronxville, New York. In between book signings, literary club meetings, and lectures, she personally answered more than three hundred cards and letters she received weekly about Custer and their life together. She remained an outspoken advocate for his integrity. She praised his military career and always placed the blame for his death and that of his company on Benteen and Reno. She lived to preserve his memory.[38]

Elizabeth worked tirelessly on the details involved with erecting statues of Custer on his grave in New York; in New Rumley, Ohio, where he was born; and in Monroe, Michigan, where he was raised. In 1881, she traveled to Kansas City, Missouri, to attend the unveiling of a painting of Custer and his men called *Custer's Last Rally*, by prominent artist John Mulvany. In November 1886, she was in the audience at Madison Square Garden with widows Annie Yates and Nettie Smith to watch a reenactment of the Battle of the Little Bighorn performed by Buffalo Bill Cody and his talented troupe of riders and sharpshooters. According to the November 7, 1886, edition of the *New York Times*, Cody had "secured the services of Curly, who was General Custer's scout at the battle and massacre of the Little Bighorn, and the Indian warrior known as Chief Gall, who led the hostiles on that day." Elizabeth loved Cody's portrayal of her husband and encouraged her friends to see the show.[39]

To further memorialize her husband's military accomplishments, Elizabeth contributed several articles to the *New York Sun, Century Magazine,* and *Lippincott's Magazine.* In a letter dated June 3, 1899, Harrison S. Morris, editor of *Lippincott's Magazine,* gave Elizabeth instructions on how to write the article they were requesting she pen. Morris wanted a three-thousand-word "genial conversational paper, full of live facts and gossip; anecdotes on women's influence in army life; what she does, of course, but what she potentially stands for or accomplished by being a soldier's wife, either officer or private. The thing should be picturesque, giving personal hardship, courtship, gallantries (with personal anecdotes), saving of life, but not hospital service. In short, the army through a woman's eyes, or something such."[40]

Elizabeth fulfilled Morris's request and then some, writing about garrison life, plains living, buffalo hunting, and the people she and Custer had met during their travels.

In the evenings when Elizabeth had put away writing assignments and responded to civic leaders and school administrators requesting that she speak at various meetings and assemblies, she sat quietly in her home studying the letters she received from supporters of her husband. "All these letters remind me how much I still miss George," she wrote to Nettie Smith in November 1887. One of the letters she was referring to came from a woman who simply referred to herself as a "Baltimore American."[41]

I had never seen General Custer's wife when I met him at the Union League club reception last winter, nor himself but once before in my life. Observing, while he was engaged in conversation, that he smiled toward a lady who had previously excited my interest. "General, who is that lady? She has such a bright, sweet look, and though so simply dressed (she wore a plain dark silk), is so thoroughly a lady that I want to know her. Above all she looks interesting and happy. I wonder who she is?"[42]

"Madam," replied the general, looking much pleased, "I shall be most happy to present the lady to you, although indeed, she knows you already," and stepping to her side he said: "Allow me to present my wife."

That is how I became acquainted with Mrs. General Custer, and, indeed, she was a wife to be fond of and proud of. Never away from her husband, all her married life was spent on the frontier which afforded no hardships or privations to her which could be compared to a separation from him. She had the sweetest, truest face, and her eyes met his with such absolute trust as thrilled me with pleasure that was plain to see.[43]

Among the many mementos around the home that reminded Elizabeth of Custer was a lock of his hair sent to her from a member of the burial detail on June 28, 1876.[44]

Unlike some of the other widows, such as Maggie Calhoun, who continued to seek out more information about their husbands, wanting to know the condition of the body when found, if their deaths were quick, or if they suffered, Elizabeth was satisfied with the limited details she'd been given. As the years passed, soldiers who had served with Custer and were with him prior to the Battle of the Little Bighorn wrote letters to his widow with news about the hours leading up to the fight.[45]

In a letter dated February 3, 1911, Custer's orderly, John Burkman, offered an account of his time with the General. The account runs from the morning of June 24, 1876, through to the point where Custer ordered Burkman to stay with the horses.[46]

> *On the day of the 24th of June 1876, after making a short march, we had coffee and proceeded on the march again that night. It was so dark you could not see your hand in front of you. As near as I could judge, it was between eleven and twelve o'clock when we unsaddled. When all was quiet, the General came to me and asked, "Where are our horses, Burkman?" I replied, "Right there." He asked me where I was going to sleep. I answered, "Right on the picket pins." He said, "That's right. We may need them before morning."*
>
> *I kept my eye on him. He crept into some brush about ten feet from me, lay down, and went to sleep. Early the next morning, the*

General Custer's orderly, John Burkman
COURTESY OF THE NATIONAL PARK SERVICE,
LITTLE BIGHORN BATTLEFIELD NATIONAL
MONUMENT, LIBI_00019_00175, PHOTOGRAPHED
BY ORLANDO SCOTT GOFF, CIRCA 1877

cook came to me and asked where the General was. I showed him where he was lying, and the General asked him for breakfast.

While in a dry creek bottom eating breakfast, two of the scouts came in from Lieutenant Varnum from the front. One of them was Isaiah Dorman, the other a Ree Indian. I showed them where they were eating breakfast. When Isaiah handed the General the message, I know he didn't finish his breakfast. He came up to me saying, "Burkman, who is that Sergeant who is carrying the regimental colors and what company does he belong to?"[47]

"It is Sergeant Victory of F Company."

"Do you know where he is?"

"Yes, Sir. He and the trumpeter are lying over there."

"Go and wake him and tell him to saddle up and go around and notify every company commander to load up their pack animals at once. But never mind. I'll go myself. Saddle up my horse."

While in the act of saddling he asked me, "What horse are you going to give me?"

I answered, "Dandy."

He said, "That's right. I didn't ride him a great ways last night."

We marched along; it must have been close to twelve o'clock when the General halted the command under a big hill. He then put Colonel Custer on guard saying, "Do not let a man or a horse on this hill while I am gone as I am going out to bring Lieutenant Varnum and his scouts in."[48]

It might have been all of a half hour when they all returned. The General gave orders to the chief trumpeter to sound officers' call once and low. He started to tell them what he had discovered, but he missed Captain McDougal. "Orderly, you go back, give my compliments to Captain McDougal, and tell him he is wanted here."[49]

He then went on to tell them what he had discovered. He had a full view of the camp and told them there was plenty there for all of us. He said, "I didn't intend to attack this camp until tomorrow morning, but we are discovered, and if we don't go and fight, they will come and fight us. The sooner we get through, the sooner we will have rest. Now as you report your companies to me, you will march the balance of the day."

Before the General rode on, he decided to ride Vic instead. He ordered me to stay with the mounts. This time when he rode off, it was the last time I saw the General. Later I begged his nephew, Arthur Reed, to remain back with me, for I would rather have taken my chances in the front.[50]

Elizabeth often wrote to the women in the widows' circle about the difficulty she'd had falling asleep since the night she had learned Custer had been killed. The cards, notes, and other correspondence that would arrive every day until she died helped to get her through those evenings when the possibility of sleep completely eluded her.

Elizabeth and friends just prior to the Battle of the Little Bighorn
COURTESY OF THE STATE HISTORICAL SOCIETY OF NORTH DAKOTA, C1060-00001

CHAPTER NINE

Broken Souls

NEWS OF THE BATTLE OF THE LITTLE BIGHORN AND CUSTER'S DEFEAT
outraged people from Virginia City, Montana, to Fayette, Missouri.
Meetings were called in hamlets across the West to organize companies
of volunteers who were ready to go to war against the Sioux. Newspaper
articles, such as one in the July 7, 1876, edition of the *St. Louis Republican*,
attempted to encourage would-be soldiers to wait before making a move
until survivors of the incident could share exactly what had occurred at
the battle.[1]

*It's enough now to know that our brave fellows were largely out-
numbered; that they assaulted a natural fortress and ambuscade
combined; and that the foe they met was well supplied with arms and
ammunition and fought desperately until victory converted fighting
into butchery. Those who have heretofore questioned the ability of the
Sioux to stand hot lead and cold steel, now have abundant reason to
change their opinion.[2]*

*The Indian war, so long talked of, has at last begun. That it will
be protracted and bitter, demanding heavy expenditures of money
and blood, its opening scene clearly proves. The Sioux, encouraged by
an unexpected triumph, which has given them an ample stock of the
best military material, will seek for and probably gain reinforcements
from other tribes. Without those reinforcements they can, if all their
bands unite, put into the field from five to seven thousand warriors.
Such a force, scattered over a wide extent of country, abounding in*

places difficult of access and capable of stout defense, will be hard to exterminate.

The Sioux are perfectly aware of what is in store for them and will prepare for it. If die they must, we may be assured they will die "game." This is not the time to speak of the causes which have brought on the conduct now fairly inaugurated. Suffice to say that we believe it might have been honorably avoided by a strict fulfillment of the treaty obligations of the federal government. But be this as it may, all, we think, will agree with us in declaring that the gold of the Black Hills, be it ever so plentiful, is not worth the fearful price already paid for it by the sacrifice of Custer and his comrades.[3]

For many who read about the deaths of Custer and his men, their thoughts and concerns were less about how to settle things with the Sioux and more on the women and children left widows and orphans. More than twenty-four women and twice that number of children were made financially destitute because of the Battle of the Little Bighorn, uncertain of where to look for help. The small pension due the grieving wives and offspring would take months to be processed and distributed. Relief would be needed sooner rather than later for women and children to start life anew away from Fort Abraham Lincoln and the army. Officers, soldiers, sailors, and others made aware of the devastation gladly contributed to various funds established to help the widowed ones. Their contributions and letters of intent were posted in the *Army and Navy Journal.*[4]

Philadelphia—July 31, 1876. "In response to the appeal of the Army and Navy Journal, my firm has subscribed $500 to the Abraham Lincoln Post Fund. . . . I mention this to show you that your very proper appeal has not fallen entirely upon deaf ears. . . . Yours truly, F. C. Newhall."[5]

West Point, New York—July 28, 1876. "Dear Sir: In behalf of two ladies who feel the utmost sympathy for the families of the poor soldiers slain in the dreadful massacre of the Seventh Cavalry, I enclose a small contribution toward the fund you are raising for their relief. . . . A. B. Berard."[6]

Monuments to General Custer and the men who died with him at the Battle of the
Little Bighorn
COURTESY OF THE LIBRARY OF CONGRESS, LC-DIG-STEREO-1S13722

In mid-July 1876, editors at the *New York Herald* proposed the
creation of a fund to erect a monument to those who fell with General
Custer on the Little Bighorn. They reasoned that a fund had already been
created for the widows and children and another would not be needed.
Not everyone agreed with the newspaper's proposal. "The impulse does
credit to the enterprise and the public spirit of the great newspaper, but
it is misdirected," a published letter to the editors in the July 20, 1876,
edition of the *New York Herald* read.[7]

A letter to the editor of the *London Saturday Review* posted in the
August 2, 1876, edition of the publication echoed the sentiments of the
letter to the *New York Herald* editors.[8]

"The *New York Herald* has started a subscription for a monument to
General Custer, which, it may be hoped, will take the form of a provision
for his widow. One correspondent of that journal thinks that he would
have preferred bread for her to a stone for himself, and we concur in that
opinion, particularly considering that the stone might possibly assume

some hideous shape or bear some extravagant inscription. Lately, some of our own efforts in this direction have taken the safe and useful form of scholarships or wings of hospitals. The Americans, like ourselves, are better at doing things than commemorating them. The same sensible writer who prefers bread to stone remarks that during the late war many officers were complimented with swords when their children needed shoes."[9]

In addition to the financial contributions made by military personnel and private citizens, moved by the tremendous loss the widows and children suffered, came donations from students and professors at military academies and inmates at Alcatraz Prison.* On September 18, 1876, inmates held a variety show for the benefit of the widows and orphans of the Custer massacre. According to the program handed out at the event, the entertainment was "both musical, and dramatic, and terpsichorean." More than $80 was raised for the cause.[10]

The October 23, 1876, edition of the *Army and Navy Journal* notified readers that the total amount donated in a four-month period to help widows and orphans of the officers and men of the Seventh Cavalry added up to more than $10,000. "This liberal contribution has come from the following sources," the *Army and Navy Journal* acknowledged:[11]

1st from generous patriotic people in civil life; 2nd from enlisted men in the Army; 3rd from commissioned officers in the Army and Navy. A portion of this has been already expended to meet immediate necessities, and it is intended to at once make final disposition of the remainder. The plan of distribution decided up on [sic] is to conform very nearly to the ratio according to rank and established by the pension laws, which gives officers of the rank of lieutenant-colonel or over $30, to majors $25, to captains $20, to 1st lieutenants $17, and 2nd lieutenants $15, and to enlisted men, $8. Under this arrangement, all that has been received from enlisted men, as well as all of the contributions from other sources which were specially designated by the contributors for the widows and orphans of enlisted men, falls to that

---

* Fort Alcatraz (later known as Alcatraz Island) was the military prison which housed Civil War prisoners of war and private citizens accused of treason.

class of sufferers; the remainder of the fund being divided among the families of the officers.

The pension laws also provide for the increase of the pensions of widows at the rate of $2 per month for each child under the age of sixteen years. This is one-quarter of the pension for an enlisted man, and it is proposed in distributing the widow's fund to add one-quarter to each widow's share for each child under sixteen years of age.[12]

As far as the widows of officers are concerned, we are fully informed. The names of enlisted men leaving widows and children under sixteen, as reported to us, are as follows:

Henry Door, Co. G, wife and two children. Frank Hughes, Co. L, wife and three children. A. McIlhurgey, Co. I, wife and one child. J. K. Wilkinson, Co. F, wife. John Kelly, Co. F, wife and three children. Thos. W. Way, Co. F, wife. Edwin Bobo, Co. C, wife and two children. Jer. Finley, Co. C, wife and two children. Robert Hughes, Co. K, wife and three children. John Mitchell, Co. I, wife and two children. Fred Hohemeyer, Co. E, wife and three children. Thos. McElroy, Co. E, wife and one child. Wm. B. Crisfield, Co. L, wife and three children.

In default of further information, the distribution of the portion of the funds set apart from enlisted men will be confined to the families of these men. Every precaution will be taken to see that the money reaches the proper hands, and, with full appreciation of the confidence shown in this most generous response to our appeal on behalf of the widows and fatherless, we shall have a care to see that the subscribers to the fund are fully informed as to its distribution. When the occasion comes to discharge ourselves finally of this trust, we expect to furnish, whatever subscriber has the right to ask, a full and exact accounting, properly certified to.[13]

In August of 1876, Elizabeth Custer was asked to furnish a list of widows and orphans to whom the funds were to be distributed. She did so, and in November checks were issued. The portions of the funds received by the officers' wives were as follows:

Mrs. Annie Yates and three children—$1,050

Mrs. Elizabeth Custer—$900

Mrs. Eliza Porter and two children—$765

Mrs. Grace Harrington and two children—$675

Mrs. Nettie Smith—$510

Mrs. Molly McIntosh—$510

Mrs. Maggie Calhoun—$510

The widows of the enlisted men were each given a check for $200, and each child received $50.[14]

Another gathering of Seventh Cavalry officers and their wives at the Custers' quarters at Fort Lincoln; Elizabeth Custer is standing at the top row, nearest the porch railing, and Margaret Calhoun is seated next to her.
COURTESY OF THE STATE HISTORICAL SOCIETY OF NORTH DAKOTA, 00091-00545

Elizabeth and the other widows were quick to send letters of appreciation to the editors of the *Army and Navy Journal*, and those letters were subsequently published in the paper.

"I can find no words suitable to express my appreciation of the evidence I have received of the sympathy of the Army and Navy," Elizabeth Custer wrote on November 28, 1876. "When the heart feels deeply, words come slowly and seem constrained and cold. I can only beg you, through the medicine of your paper, to thank them for me in your own language."[15]

On December 2, 1876, Annie Yates wrote, "I am totally unable to put in language my gratitude and appreciation for this noble evidence of a nation's tribute to our bereavement, but I must express my thanks, even though the expression may be faint in comparison with what I feel. I also bear in mind to whom we owe the promoting of this generous gift and realize the labor and anxiety you must have had in taking charge of so large a benefaction.[16]

"Accept my sincere thanks for the delicate manner in which you have attended to this mission, and if you will kindly express for me my heartfelt appreciation to those who have so generously befriended us, you will add to your other great acts of kindness."[17]

Maggie Calhoun also sent a letter of gratitude dated December 5, 1876. "Will you please convey to the many friends to whom I am indebted my heartfelt thanks for the kind and generous testimonial of their sympathy of which I have been the recipient," she wrote. "My delay in acknowledging the receipt thereof has been unavoidable, which I trust you will pardon. Allow me to thank you for the interest you have manifested in our behalf."[18]

When pensions for the women and children who lost their husbands and fathers at the Little Bighorn were finally issued, enlisted men's wives received $8 a month, and each of their dependents received $2 a month. Officers' wives received $17 to $40 a month, with their children receiving $18 to $22 a month.[19]

Life after the death of their beloved spouses was a struggle for the widowed ones, some more so than others. Annie Gibson Yates remained at her home in Monroe, Michigan, until the passing of her father, William Milnor Roberts, in July 1881. Annie then moved to Carlisle, Pennsylvania, with her children and settled in the house where she was raised. William Roberts had left a small inheritance for his daughter, and she combined that with the modest army pension she had been awarded to get by. In June 1888, Congress approved an increase in her pension from $20 a month to $40 a month.[20]

Annie supplemented her income as a private tutor. An advertisement in the October 6, 1881, edition of the *Carlisle Weekly Herald* informed students interested in improving their singing techniques how she could be of service. "Mrs. Annie Y. Yates, a pupil of Mademoiselle Gubert, of Perelli's School, Phila., Pa., will give instruction in Vocal Music, at her residence, No. 7 South Pitt Street. Terms per quarter (20 lessons) $12. Two test lessons given free of charge. Particular attention to breathing and to a correct style of pronunciation in English, French, or Italian."[21]

Annie was a devoted mother who spent as much time as she could with her three children. She made sure they remained close with Elizabeth Custer and the other Little Bighorn widows in their circle. The Yates family spent every Christmas holiday with Elizabeth in New York, where Custer's widow lived. Elizabeth doted on Annie's children and, as she was the godmother of the oldest Yates boy, took a particular interest in his future. At her recommendation, she worked to gain an appointment to West Point for George Yates, but it was not to be. He attended the Dickinson College Preparatory School in Carlisle and went on to attend Lehigh University in South Bethlehem in Pennsylvania. George eventually became an executive with the New York Telephone Company, married, and purchased a home in Brooklyn.[22]

Annie's daughter, Bessie, became a registered nurse. She was married on September 4, 1907, to a lawyer named Hugh N. Hewson, and the couple made their home in Mount Vernon, New York.[23]

Milnor, the youngest of the Yates children, was placed in the Pennsylvania Training School for Feeble-Minded Children when he was sixteen years old. He suffered a stroke in October 1895 and died from pneumonia the following year, on July 15.[24]

Annie relocated to New York in 1910 to be close to Bessie, George, and her grandchildren. On December 9, 1914, Annie was killed in a tragic accident. The December 10, 1914, edition of *The Sentinel* explained what happened.[25]

Caught in a manner not yet explained as she was entering the rear car of the subway local train at Fourteenth Street, Mrs. Annie Gibson Yates, sixty-five years old, a wealthy widow of No. 82 Pierrepont Street, Brooklyn, suffered injuries which caused her death a few hours later in Bellevue Hospital at nine o'clock last night.

Although the platform was crowded at the time of the accident, police were unable to find anyone who witnessed it. William Siegel, of No. 121 St. Mark's Place, and Thomas Ryan of No. 120 West Ninety-Seventh Street, saw the woman as she was being rolled between the platform and car and as she fell unconscious upon the rails when the train released her. They jumped down and lifted her to the platform.

Mrs. Yates left her home in Brooklyn on a shopping tour and she left the express train at Fourteenth Street with the idea of taking the local train for Twenty-third Street. It is presumed that her dress was caught by some projection. Her skull and arms were fractured. The woman's identity was established by means of cards found in her handbag.[26]

Annie's remains were sent back to Carlisle, Pennsylvania, and her funeral services were held at St. Patrick's Catholic Church on December 12, 1914. She was remembered as a "woman of great culture and brilliant attainment who was a favorite in literary and artistic circles in New York City."[27]

For several years after the Battle of the Little Bighorn, Margaret Calhoun contented herself with remaining in Monroe, Michigan, and caring for her grieving parents. Her mother, Maria, who had struggled with poor health since the death of her three sons in June 1876, succumbed to her illnesses on January 14, 1882. Margaret watched over her father,

Reverend Emanuel Custer, until early 1883, when she decided to pursue a career in reader's theater. She traveled to Detroit to study dramatic elocution, and, upon graduating, began presenting select readings at churches and libraries throughout Kansas and Missouri.[28]

For more than two years, she toured the country, drawing large crowds at each of her public appearances. She was an exceptional dramatic reader, and newspapers everywhere she went praised her work. "The admirers of the talent of Mrs. Margaret Custer Calhoun, and they include all who have ever come within the charm of her voice and presence, will be afforded an evening's enjoyment on next Tuesday, the 23rd, when she appears in the Opera House," the October 17, 1888, edition of the *Carlisle Weekly Herald* read.[29]

"She is a magnetic and versatile elocutionist, and her selections, varied in character, offer a wide range for a display of the dramatic, the pathetic, and humorous. She is not a stranger in our midst, having given a public recital here a year or more ago when she completely captivated her audience, and she has enlivened many a private gathering by her accommodating and ever ready disposition to entertain."[30]

In November 1885, Elizabeth tried to persuade Margaret to consider accepting an appointment as pension agent in Detroit. It was a position initially offered to Elizabeth, but she suggested her sister-in-law would be better suited for the job. She knew Margaret often grew tired of traveling and thought the job would provide stability. Margaret declined the appointment but, in 1891, did decide to give up life on the road for a brief time. The widow Calhoun was given the job as head librarian at the state library in Lansing, Michigan. She left the position in the spring of 1893 to return to performing.[31]

Margaret would often accept offers to deliver dramatic readings in the New York area where Elizabeth lived. She enjoyed spending time with her sister-in-law and visiting with the other widows in their circle. More than fifteen years after the tragic event that cost them their husbands, the women still longed for the men they had lost and felt comfortable sharing their grief. "I've not ever been, nor am I able still, to forget the lingering touch of his hand in mine," Margaret wrote Elizabeth from a hotel in Atlanta in September 1895, where she was to perform at the

Atlanta Exposition. "I still long for him, mourn for him, through all the dark and lonely hours."[32]

Like all of the other widows, Margaret could not have survived solely on the pension the military gave her. The House of Representatives met on February 21, 1898, to vote to increase the pension amount she had been getting, from $17 a month to $30.[33]

Using a portion of the money she had saved from performing public readings, along with the extra pension funds she was now receiving, Margaret was able to purchase a home for herself. She and widow Nettie Smith pooled their money and bought seven lots at the corner of Jericho and Willis Avenues in Brooklyn, for $1,000.[34]

Shortly after buying property on which to build her future home, Margaret met a contractor named John H. Maugham, with the Ferguson Construction Company, and the two fell in love. The couple was married on July 5, 1903, at Onteora Park in Hunter, New York. The newlyweds were happily living together in their New York apartment on West 103rd Street and contemplating trips to South America and Europe when Margaret became ill and was diagnosed with stomach cancer.[35]

Margaret was being cared for by reputable medical physicians for more than a year when she decided to forego their treatment. She chose, instead, to get help from various Christian Science healers and nurses. She died from the disease on March 22, 1910. Margaret's husband had her body taken to Monroe, Michigan, where she was laid to rest beside her brothers, mother, and father. She was fifty-eight years old when she passed away.[36]

Molly McIntosh returned to Baltimore after her husband's death. She lived with her mother and rarely interacted with anyone outside her family and the other widowed ones. Her mother passed away in 1879, and Molly became even more isolated from the world. According to her sister Katherine Gibson's memoirs, "Mollie had been so prostrated with grief that she recoiled from any further contact with the army." Elizabeth Custer worried about her friend and wrote her several letters encouraging her to "find a reason to continue on." It wasn't until the winter of 1883 that she found a renewed sense of purpose.

"Some years later [Molly] suddenly changed her mind," Katherine wrote about her sister's transformation.[37] "The reason for it was the anticipated advent into this vale of tears of our first and, as fate decreed it, only child. When I received her wire announcing that she was already en route to join me, I mentally quailed, recalling her quaint antipathy to boy babies. 'Champion bawlers and devilish brats,' she dubbed them with a sniff. Suppose I had one! I pictured her figuratively slapping the unfortunate infant in the face with her sunbonnet, like Betsey Trotwood [the fictional character in Charles Dickens's novel *David Copperfield*], and quitting us in high dudgeon.

"Anyway, she left the train at Fort Pierre and, in December, in 30 degrees below zero weather, battled by way of stagecoach through ice and snow to Fort Meade, arriving in time for the great event. However, when she gathered my two-and-a-half-pound baby girl in her capable arms, rolled her in an army blanket, and began issuing spritely orders to everyone, Frank [Katherine's husband] included, I knew that all was well."[38]

Molly's niece, Kate, lovingly referred to her as "My Auntie Tosh." For a short time, the little girl did wonders for the grief-stricken widow. When Molly's sister Katherine and her new daughter Kate left the Dakota Territory to travel to Philadelphia for the funeral of Katherine's mother-in-law, Molly sank back into a dark depression. She returned to Baltimore, and there she stayed. In 1909, she had her husband's remains exhumed from the cemetery at Fort Leavenworth and reinterred at the Arlington National Cemetery. Molly died on May 12, 1910, and was laid to rest beside her husband.[39]

The life Molly and Donald shared made the news in 1995 when the lieutenant's wedding ring was found near the marker where his body was discovered on the Little Bighorn battlefield. Inscribed inside the band of the gold ring with a small diamond in the Old European–cut style were the initials "DD" and "MM" and the year "66," which referred to the year 1866, in which the McIntoshes were married. The wedding ring was later sold at auction for $18,750.00.[40]

Henrietta "Nettie" Smith followed much the same course as Molly. After burying her husband, Captain Algernon Smith, at Fort Leavenworth,

Kansas, in 1877, Nettie returned to her parents' home in Herkimer County, New York. When she wasn't caring for her father and mother, Hezekiah and Mary, or visiting with Elizabeth Custer in Lawrence Park, New York, she was maintaining a scrapbook she had put together about her husband and the other men who died at the Little Bighorn. Among the clippings included in the scrapbook were poems about the Battle of the Little Bighorn by Walter Carey and Henry Wadsworth Longfellow, interviews with General Terry, Marcus Reno, and Frederick Benteen, and photographs of the slain soldiers at Fort Abraham Lincoln.[41]

Nettie saved several articles about the long friendship she and Elizabeth had enjoyed. The articles noted the bond the pair had forged, along with the other widows, because of the tragic event in Montana. "We have been a truly sad party," Nettie wrote in a letter to Elizabeth in March 1901. "But how much more sorrowful we would have been without one another's company. For whom else could truly know the relentless ache for the men taken from us?"[42]

Nettie Smith died on June 16, 1903, at the age of sixty. She was buried at the Newport Cemetery next to her mother, who had passed away in 1896, and her father, who had passed away in 1902.[43]

Like all of the other widowed ones, Eliza Porter was deeply affected by the news of her husband's fate. She left Fort Abraham Lincoln with her two sons, David and James, and traveled to Maine to be near her family. When Eliza's youngest son James died in December 1876, she focused solely on her remaining son. On more than one occasion, Eliza took David with her to visit Elizabeth Custer and the other widows in New York.[44]

In 1890, shortly after David graduated from high school, he moved to Berkeley, California, to attend the University of California. Eliza moved west when David completed his college degree and found work as a mining engineer. He married and had two children. For a time, Eliza lived with her son, daughter-in-law, and grandchildren. On April 17, 1903, David died suddenly from heart disease.[45]

According to the May 1, 1903, edition of the *Berkeley Daily Gazette*, David had been working extremely hard as a county surveyor for a mine in Idaho. "At the time of his death he was in New Jersey, finishing some mine engineering work," the article noted. "He was living in a cabin with some other engineers who heard him breathing heavily on the night of his death, as though he was suffering from a nightmare. Nothing was thought of the incident, however, until the body of Porter was found dead in bed the next morning."[46]

At about sixty-seven years of age, Eliza Porter died on December 13, 1915, after struggling with an unknown illness. She was buried at the Alta Mesa Memorial Park in Santa Clara, California.[47] Throughout the course of her life as a widow she often discussed writing a book about her frontier experiences. She wanted to pass her story along to her grandchildren. Elizabeth Custer and Annie Yates discouraged her from recalling the past because of the way sad memories affected her.

Grace Harrington never accepted the fact that her husband had died at the Little Bighorn. She was haunted by the notion he was alive and being held captive by renegade Indians who refused to return to the reservations.

Grace dreamed he had been traded from one rogue tribe to another, that he was seriously hurt and hungry, and that he wasn't physically able to make it back to her and their children. Her inability to cope prompted her physician to prescribe chloral hydrate, a potent sedative and hypnotic drug. The medicine acted as a depressant with Grace and made the nightmares she had about Lieutenant Harrington much more frequent.[48]

During her waking hours, she wrote letters to politicians and military officials requesting that search parties return to Montana to look for Henry. No one was willing to commit troops or time to the venture. Emotionally exhausted and frustrated by the lack of support for what she was convinced had to be done, Grace set out on her own to find her soldier husband.[49] The last anyone saw of her was on February 13, 1885. She had traveled from Highland Falls, New York, to Fort Worth, Texas, to meet with her sister, Mrs. Minnie Matthews. A station agent for the Missouri Pacific Railroad remembered seeing her and mentioned she was acting "strangely." When the agent asked her where she was going, she told him she was headed to the Eufaula, Indian Territory. The agent then inquired what she was going to do there. Grace replied with a laugh that she didn't know.[50]

Grace's siblings hired detectives to help locate their sister. They hoped she would find her way to one of the other women in the widows' circle, but, by October 1885, neither Elizabeth Custer nor any of the other widows had heard from her. The detectives were unsuccessful in their search and had given up the hunt by the end of the year. Nancy Harrington, Grace's mother-in-law, had petitioned the court for guardianship of Grace's son and daughter. The May 4, 1886, edition of the *Coldwater Republican* reported that the widow had not drawn on the $15 a month pension granted her during her absence. Arrangements were made for the children to claim the funds.[51]

On December 2, 1887, more than two years after Grace had been reported missing, a telegram was sent from Minnie Matthews in Fort Worth to her family in New York informing them that Grace had finally been located. An article in the December 10, 1887, edition of the

Survivors and their wives returned to the Little Bighorn in 1886 to pay their respects.
COURTESY OF THE DENVER PUBLIC LIBRARY, SPECIAL COLLECTIONS

Chattanooga Commercial explained the circumstances around Grace's reappearance. The article was one that initially ran in the Fort Worth newspaper after an interview with Minnie.[52]

As far as Mrs. Harrington can remember . . . she was walking along the streets of Dallas when she was approached by a policeman, who took hold of her arm and asked her if she was drunk, at which she laughed and passed on. She also remembers purchasing a ticket at a railroad office for Eufaula, a small town on the Missouri, Kansas, and Texas road, but has no recollection of going to that place from Dallas yet remembers being there for some time.[53]

What she did there or how long she remained she cannot tell. It appears that her mind was a blank and that her memory revived only at intervals widely apart. The next account she gives of herself is that she was walking along a railroad track in a country where she never saw a horse or a living thing and says that she well remembers walking on a high framework that spanned a wide stream and then all was a blank.

She next remembers being in a house in Gainesville, where she was engaged in some menial work for the family but does not remember who the family was. While there a lady whose face was familiar to her remarked to the lady of the house that she knew Mrs. Harrington when she was the wife of an army officer. Beyond this the wanderer could recollect nothing of her life in Gainesville. It was in Fort Worth when the next ray of light broke upon her clouded mind, and she says she wandered about the streets of this city for many days doing she knows not what. The next account she gives of herself was in Marshall, Texas, where she says she was a chambermaid in a large hotel. From there she went to Texarkana, and says she was there a long time, but cannot tell what she was doing.[54]

From Texarkana, according to her story, she wandered to Arkansas and lived first in one town and then in another, doing drudgery work in private families and in hotels. She was in Arkadelphia, or near there, cooking for a railroad outfit, and, indeed, it seems that she never engaged in any work except that of a menial character.

One of the last views Elizabeth Custer and the other widows had of Fort Lincoln, from the east bank of the Missouri River
COURTESY OF THE STATE HISTORICAL SOCIETY OF NORTH DAKOTA, A1626-00001

It was at the little town of Whitesboro that she first recollected or thought of home and children. A ray of light struck her mind, and she recalled everything. She wrote to her sister, Mrs. Matthews, directing her to come and get her.[55]

Minnie Matthews escorted her sister back to her home in Fort Worth. Newspaper correspondents, made aware when the sisters returned to Texas, flocked to the Matthews' residence seeking to interview the unfortunate widow. Minnie informed the reporters that Grace's health was bad and that doctors had advised she be sent away to recover from the ordeal. She would not allow them to see her but shared what she could about her sister's struggles.

"Oh, it was a terrible sight," Minnie told the journalists. "When my sister left home, she was only thirty-seven years old, and it was not quite three years since she had changed to be a woman who looked twenty years older. I didn't recognize her at first. It wasn't until she exclaimed, 'Minnie, don't you know me?' We got her some different clothes and will be sending her south in hope this will be beneficial for her health."[56]

In time, Grace's physical health was fully restored. Reuniting with her children helped improve her mental state, but she never completely regained the memory of her time away from her home and loved ones. Grace died on May 7, 1919, at the age of seventy. She never stopped believing Henry was a captive of the Indians or that he would come home to her. She was laid to rest at the West Point Military Academy Post Cemetery.[57]

One by one, the widows of the officers who fell with General Custer at the Little Bighorn passed away, until only Elizabeth Custer remained, the one who kept the widows connected.

CHAPTER TEN

Last to Go

PERSISTENT RAINDROPS TAPPED AGAINST THE WINDOWS OF ELIZABETH Custer's Park Avenue apartment in New York City. The prim, eighty-four-year-old woman, clad in a black, Edwardian dress, stared out at the dreary, foggy weather. She wore a pensive expression. Her graying hair was pulled back neatly into a tight bun, although a few loose tendrils had escaped and gently framed her small face. Her throat was modestly covered with lace.

The room around Elizabeth was grand in size and filled with items she had collected during her days on the Western Plains. Framed drawings of the Kansas prairie, a trunk with George's initials across the top, photographs of friends and family at various outposts, and an assortment of books on subjects ranging from travel beyond the Mississippi to the types of wildflowers that lined the Oregon Trail were among her treasures. The sparse furnishings in the apartment were covered with newspapers and journals. A small desk was littered with hundreds of letters.

Elizabeth glanced at the clock on a nearby table and then clicked on a radio housed in the gigantic cabinet beside her. As she tuned the dial through static and tones, a bright, maroon light from the console of the radio sifted into the hollow of the dark room. At the same time, the fog outside the window lifted a bit, and the vague, misty outlines of palatial apartment buildings, museums, and churches came into view.

Elizabeth found the radio station she was looking for and leaned back in a plush chair as a voice described upcoming programming. She pulled a shawl around her shoulders and sat, patiently waiting. After a few moments, an announcer broke in with pertinent information about the broadcast to which Elizabeth planned to listen: an episode of *Frontier Fighters* entitled "Custer's Last Stand." The airdate was June 26, 1926, fifty years after the Battle of the Little Bighorn.[1]

As the audio reenactment unfolded, Elizabeth contemplated all that had occurred in the last five decades. All of her fellow widowed ones had passed, and there was no one left to discuss the bygone days—those who had been there throughout the good and horrific times. There remained no friends who knew, as she did, the trials and hardships endured by tenderly nurtured young women who had braved winds and blizzards, mosquitoes and heat to be near the men they loved.[2]

Elizabeth Custer's home in Westchester County, New York
COURTESY OF THE WESTCHESTER COUNTY HISTORICAL SOCIETY, WCHS0263

Elizabeth Custer had made a life for herself beyond the tragic death of her husband, but not without his omnipresent memory shaping her every decision. Her identity was tied to General Custer's career, and she made no apologies for that. She had traveled back and forth across the United States numerous times speaking to the public about Custer and their life together. Her reputation as a stalwart widow and author of American tales of frontier life made her a suitable candidate as an unofficial ambassador for the United States in foreign countries. She visited Europe, the Far East, Egypt, and Turkey, keeping detailed journals of her adventures. The journals included swatches of fabric from traditional garments and drawings of ancient ruins and the people who inhabited the lands. She was well received everywhere she went. No matter where she traveled, she never strayed far from the topic of her infamous husband. She was his champion and took on any author who dared publish a book that cast Custer in a negative light.[3]

Years after the Battle of the Little Bighorn, Elizabeth received letters from men who had served with Custer and had fond memories of him. In the summer of 1920, a letter from Allendale Station dated June 14 was delivered to her home. The seventy-two-year-old man who penned the letter claimed to have been "one of the General's men when we marched from the Powder River to the Little Big Horn." The former soldier also wrote, "I still see General Custer and the old Glorious flag of the Seventh Cavalry flying next to him as he rode to battle. I just send a few lines and loving regards for the great General and officer who deserves to always be remembered.[4]

"I was sorry for the ladies left at Fort Lincoln, for what they lost and how their lives were reduced because of that loss. I was wounded in the head and could not stay with the others. I was moved to the steamer *Far West*. If I could, I would have been with the General on the hill."[5]

In addition to letters from supportive soldiers, Elizabeth received invitations to special events commemorating the Battle of the Little Bighorn. In 1889, a massive, panoramic painting, called a cyclorama, of Custer and his men at the last fight was installed at a museum in Boston, Massachusetts. The proprietors of the Boston Cyclorama Company hosting the exhibit at a museum on Tremont Street wanted Elizabeth

General George Armstrong Custer

to attend the opening event and "give her opinion of the correctness of detail." Mrs. Custer kindly declined, noting she wasn't qualified to comment on the battle. "I cannot summon the courage to visit the cyclorama . . . as you request me to do . . . ," she kindly explained to the exhibitor. "But I am extremely grateful that you have chosen a subject which commemorates in pictorial history my husband's career."[6]

Included in Elizabeth's response to the Boston Cyclorama Company were choice remarks about those who continued to condemn her husband for his actions that day.

Criticism of the battle has often been offered by men who have never had experience in Indian warfare, but the most distinguished Indian fighter we now have, reminds those who question General Custer's dividing his troops in the attack, that in the battle of Washita he followed the same course with great success. The same officer has told me that in fighting all the other tribes he found none to compare with the Sioux as warriors; but adds that he would rather fight the whole Sioux nation than the critics and enemies in his rear.[7]

The friends of the Indians have questioned the right of our Government to organize an expedition like that of the spring of 1876;

A scene from Custer's Last Fight in the Boston Cyclorama Company presentation
COURTESY OF THE LIBRARY OF CONGRESS, LC-USZ61-26

but Bishop Whipple, whose philanthropic work among the tribes has been so indefatigable, sent me a message after the battle that assured me he felt Chief Gall's band needed punishing. He said that in spite of every effort made to induce the Indians to come on to a reservation, they had refused and meanwhile committed depredations not only on white settlers but on neighboring tribes.[8]

Included in the letter Elizabeth sent to the people staging the exhibit was a treasured picture of Custer and one of his swords. These items were on loan to the facility until the show concluded.

The Boston event wasn't the first—nor the last—time Elizabeth was asked to take part in a program to honor those military men who died at the Little Bighorn. In 1921, Montana state officials hoped she would join them in a celebration at the forty-fifth anniversary of the battle. She had never visited the spot where her husband met his end. Ultimately, she could not bring herself to attend, but sent a memento instead. According to the June 13, 1921, edition of the *Billings Gazette*:

Quite an object of curiosity is being displayed at the Carnegie County library since its arrival here the fore part of this week. It is the buckskin suit worn by General Custer during the campaigns in Montana and the Dakotas. The suit is of the typical pioneer day style—light yellow in color, close fitting with leather fringe protruding from the seams, made of elk skin treated to a velvety finish. The suit is very well preserved and will doubtless remain so for decades to come. The donor of this priceless relic is Mrs. Elizabeth Custer, widow of the general, and she expresses her notice of making this gift to Big Horn County people in the following letter.[9]

"I am sending one of my choicest possessions to the library at Hardin—the general's buckskins . . . I did not attempt to have anything done to them for I thought it would appeal to the loyal people who are doing so much to make June 25 a success if I sent them as they are—showing what hard riding was done over those western plains.

"I am also sending pamphlets that I have prepared and had published by the Century Magazine *company and about which I will*

*write you later. I regret very much that I haven't the fortitude to be
with all of you on the 25th of June.*

"*Elizabeth Custer.*

"*P. S.—We both know how necessary it is to provide protection
against mutilation of museum articles, and I am going to ask if you
will order a plain pine box (painted, if you wish) with a glass front
for the buckskins and kindly send the bill to me.*"[10]

Elizabeth spent her declining years overseeing fund-raising efforts
for museums seeking to honor her husband and the men who died at the
Little Bighorn and taking part in charitable events such as the annual
garden party held to benefit the Army Relief Society.

Elizabeth was a supporter of the arts as well. In 1926, at the age of
eighty-four, she made a documentary entitled *The Pottery Maker*. The
film, made by the Metropolitan Museum of Art at the Greenwich House
of Pottery, featured potter Victor Raffo. In *The Pottery Maker*, Raffo's
daughter Ruth played the part of a little girl interested in the way pottery
was made, and Elizabeth portrayed her grandmother. The silent picture
was directed by actress Maude Adams.[11]

Patrons who had the pleasure of meeting Elizabeth at various
fund-raising programs often commented on how she could have been
mistaken for a woman in her sixties. She walked briskly, spoke clearly,
and could not be intimidated. At a benefit for the Brooklyn Children's
Museum on November 8, 1928, Elizabeth was poised and kind as she
greeted others at the event.[12]

"Mrs. Custer does not like publicity," a reporter covering the affair
noted. "She has been accosted by many seeking interviews in her day, and
she is quite familiar with their tactics. It is no secret that she does not like
questions when she knows that her answers are to appear in print.

"When she could be persuaded to speak, she spoke with freedom
on whatever topics arose, and for a few moments allowed her mind to
return to the days when she and her husband played the part of pioneers
of the Western Trail. 'Abraham Lincoln,' Mrs. Custer shared, (this as an
example of speaking freely on whatever topic arises) 'was always cool and
collected, even in the face of the most trying circumstances. Whereas

other men in public life at the time seemed to be constantly under pressure lest they might say something not in keeping with their position, he was always free and easy and completely unaffected.'"[13]

After waxing nostalgic over President Lincoln, Elizabeth spoke of her travels with her husband and the times she rode horseback with him seventy and eighty miles a day. According to the November 9, 1928, edition of the *Standard Union*, "her tone in reminiscing about bygone times and the man [to] whose memory she remained faithful gave evidence she still believed he was the finest who had ever lived." The fifty years that had passed since his death had not dimmed her recollection of him.[14]

At home in her Park Avenue apartment in June 1929, Elizabeth pored over mementos, pictures, and journals to begin work on a book about the Civil War. She believed the adventures and tragedies she had lived through with Custer at that time would make a good read. When she wasn't working on the book, she focused on responding to the many letters she received daily from curious veterans wanting to know about her life and details about traveling with the Seventh Cavalry.

"I feel I owe it to them," she once confessed about answering all of her correspondence. "There are so few of them left, and old soldiers are sensitive. But I find that they are very well cared for all over the country, and I am glad of that. They sent me so many stories of the campaigning days. It is amazing when you think how far back it all is."[15]

When Elizabeth ventured out, she would visit the Cosmopolitan Club near her home. She believed that club life for women was one of the most important advantages of the modern age. "I think the companionship of women in clubs is one of the greatest blessings of the day," she shared with a reporter. "In the old days one had to go visiting. But the modern club, I find, is a consolation for the widow and the old maid."[16]

Elizabeth marked each anniversary of the Battle of the Little Bighorn by doing an interview with reporters about the hazards of living on the frontier and the courage of her protector husband. On the fifty-fifth anniversary of the famous Last Stand, Elizabeth declined to speak with the press, explaining, "I am not feeling up to the mark." Her niece told them Elizabeth was tired and her health was failing.[17]

On April 2, 1933, Custer's widow suffered a heart attack. She passed away on April 4, just four days short of her ninety-first birthday. The news of her death was carried in every major publication around the world. The April 16, 1933, edition of the *Salt Lake Tribune* noted: "[I]n her passing, another link with the colorful frontier days is severed. Up to the day of her death, Mrs. Custer's recollection of the stirring days of the Indian Wars remained acute. For she was no stay-at-home soldier's wife in those days but insisted on accompanying her husband on many of his campaigns."[18]

The *San Antonio Express* echoed the sentiment, and added, "In the early [1870s], when women were making their first demands for higher education and otherwise were preparing the way for their sisters of the twentieth century, young Elizabeth Custer also pioneered. She went west with her soldier-husband to share with him the hardships, dangers and thrills of post life on the Plains."[19]

Elizabeth's close friends and relatives celebrated her life at a service held at her Park Avenue apartment. She was laid to rest next to Custer at West Point on April 6, 1933. She was remembered by many as a woman of many talents, a loving aunt, and a fiercely devoted wife.[20] She had outlived all of Custer's key critics. Marcus Reno had died on March 29, 1889, following surgery for cancer of the tongue at the

General George Custer and Elizabeth Custer
COURTESY OF THE LIBRARY OF CONGRESS, LC-DIG-CW-PBH-03130

age of fifty-four. Frederick Benteen died on June 17, 1898, of cerebral apoplexy, at sixty-four.[21]

Elizabeth's will, offered for probate on May 11, 1933, included instructions for several historic artifacts. Among the artifacts were two flags of truce used on the occasion of the surrender of General Lee at Appomattox. She left the flags to the United States government. A button owned by George Washington was left to West Point Academy.[22] Although not mentioned in the will, the May 12, 1933, edition of the *Salt Lake Tribune* reported that Elizabeth made monetary provisions for her two nieces as well.[23]

Until the moment she drew her last breath, Elizabeth maintained that Custer was a patriot and hero. "You are a positive use to your day and generation," she wrote to her husband just before the Battle of the Little Bighorn. "Do you not see that your life is precious at that account?"[24]

Notes

Chapter One: God and Time Alone

1. Frost, *General Custer's Libbie*, 232–33; *Monroe Commercial*, August 13, 1876.
2. *Monroe Commercial*, August 13, 1876; Frost, *General Custer's Libbie*, 232–33.
3. Leckie, *Elizabeth Bacon Custer and the Making of a Myth*, 217–18; Frost, *General Custer's Libbie*, 232–33; *Monroe Commercial*, August 13, 1876.
4. *Monroe Commercial*, August 13, 1876.
5. Ibid.
6. Monaghan, *The Life of General George Armstrong Custer*, 392.
7. Leighton, *The Story of General Custer*, 164–65; Merington, *The Custer Story*, 297–98; Frost, *General Custer's Libbie*, 226; Custer, *Boots and Saddles*, 216–17.
8. Custer, *Boots and Saddles*, 222.
9. Leckie, *Elizabeth Bacon Custer and the Making of a Myth*, 190; *Billings Gazette*, May 27, 1961; Fougera, *With Custer's Cavalry*, 263.
10. Fougera, *With Custer's Cavalry*, 264–65; Custer, *Boots and Saddles*, 222–24.
11. Hanson, *The Conquest of the Missouri*, 312–14.
12. Frost, *General Custer's Libbie*, 227.
13. Ibid.
14. Merington, *The Custer Story*, 307.
15. "Victorian Days: Death and Mourning," *AVictorian.com*.
16. Elizabeth Custer Collection, Chris Kortlander (private collection); Elizabeth Custer Papers Collection: OGL #1496.
17. Elizabeth Custer Collection, Chris Kortlander (private collection).
18. Ibid.
19. Ibid.
20. Ibid.
21. Ibid.
22. *Billings Gazette*, November 13, 1932.
23. Hanson, *The Conquest of the Missouri*, 314–15.
24. Ibid.
25. Johnson, *The Unregimented General: A Biography of Nelson A. Miles*, 86–87.
26. *Democrat and Chronicle*, July 20, 1876.
27. Ibid.
28. Ibid.

29. *Junction City Weekly*, August 5, 1876.

30. Leckie, *Elizabeth Bacon Custer and the Making of a Myth*, 203–05; Elizabeth Custer Collection, Chris Kortlander (private collection).

31. Elizabeth Custer Collection, Chris Kortlander (private collection).

32. Ibid.

33. *Richmond Dispatch*, July 18, 1876.

34. Ibid.

35. Elizabeth Custer Collection, Chris Kortlander (private collection).

36. *Billings Gazette*, November 13, 1932.

37. *Burlington Daily Sentinel*, August 15, 1876.

38. *Wheeling Intelligencer*, August 9, 1876.

39. *Findlay Jeffersonian*, August 4, 1876.

40. *Bismarck Weekly Tribune*, August 24, 1876.

41. *Fargo Record*, August 4, 1895.

42. *Democrat and Chronicle*, August 7, 1876; *Hope Pioneer*, December 15, 1910.

43. *Star Tribune*, August 14, 1876; Frost, *General Custer's Libbie*, 232–33.

44. Ibid.

45. Ibid.

46. "Standard Atlas of Holmes County, Ohio," *Ohio Memory Collection*; *Star Tribune*, August 14, 1876.

47. *Star Tribune*, August 14, 1876.

48. Elizabeth Custer Collection, Chris Kortlander (private collection).

49. Ibid.

50. Ibid.

51. Ibid.

52. Elizabeth Custer Collection, Chris Kortlander (private collection); Elizabeth Custer Papers Collection: OGL #1496.

53. *United States Army Journal & Gazette* (also referred to as the *Army and Navy Journal*), July 15, 1876.

54. Elizabeth Custer Collection, Chris Kortlander (private collection).

55. Ibid.

CHAPTER TWO: DUTY AND FAITHFULNESS

1. Monroe County Museum System, Local History Division: Custer Collection, Frost Collection (Box 2: Files 2-4 and 2-5); Elizabeth Custer Collection, Chris Kortlander (private collection).

2. Elizabeth Custer Collection, Chris Kortlander (private collection).

3. Ibid.

4. Ibid.

5. *Lancaster Examiner*, July 19, 1876; *New Orleans Republican*, July 16, 1876.

6. Elizabeth Custer Collection, Chris Kortlander (private collection).

7. Ibid.

8. Pohanka, *A Summer on the Plains*, 42–46.

9. Ibid.

10. Ibid.

11. Ibid., 103–04.

12. Ibid., 105.

13. Merington, *The Custer Story*, 243–44.

14. *Daily Memphis Avalanche*, April 29, 1873.

15. Pohanka, *A Summer on the Plains*, 106; *Sioux City Journal*, June 20, 1873.

16. Pohanka, *A Summer on the Plains*, 106–07.

17. Merington, *The Custer Story*, 249-50.

18. Ibid.

19. *Helena Weekly Herald*, September 11, 1873.

20. Ibid.

21. Pohanka, *A Summer on the Plains*, 107–09.

22. *Inter Ocean*, July 4, 1874.

23. Elizabeth Custer Collection, Chris Kortlander (private collection).

24. Pohanka, *A Summer on the Plains*, 109–10.

25. Ibid.

26. *Detroit Free Press*, August 11, 1874.

27. Ibid.

28. Ibid.

29. *Bismarck Tribune*, August 27, 1873.

30. Katz, *Custer in Photographs*, 49–50; *Galveston Daily News*, December 22, 1874.

31. Pohanka, *A Summer on the Plains*, 110–12.

32. Ibid.

33. Ibid.

34. Ibid.

35. Ibid.

36. Elizabeth Custer Collection, Chris Kortlander (private collection).

37. Ibid.

38. Ibid.

39. Ibid.

40. *St. Paul Tribune*, April 21, 1876.

41. Elizabeth Custer Collection, Chris Kortlander (private collection).

42. *Press & Daily Dakotan*, April 29, 1876.

43. Elizabeth Custer Collection, Chris Kortlander (private collection).

44. Pohanka, *A Summer on the Plains*, 125; *Bismarck Weekly*, May 24, 1876.

45. Pohanka, *A Summer on the Plains*, 125–26.

46. Ibid.

47. Ibid.

48. Ibid.

49. Pohanka, *A Summer on the Plains*, 127.

50. *Daily Gazette*, September 19, 1876.

51. Evans-Hatch, *Centuries Along the Upper Niobrara: Historic Resource Study*.

52. Reece, "Interment of the Custer Dead," *Friends of the Little Bighorn Battlefield*.

53. Reece, "Interment of the Custer Dead," *Friends of the Little Bighorn Battlefield*; Frost, *General Custer's Libbie*, 241–42.

CHAPTER THREE: HIDDEN AWAY

1. *Detroit Free Press*, February 22, 1891.
2. Pohanka, *A Summer on the Plains*, 167–68; Frost, *General Custer's Libbie*, 214–15.
3. Leckie, *Elizabeth Bacon Custer and the Making of a Myth*, 217–18; Frost, *General Custer's Libbie*, 123–24.
4. Hatch, *The Last Days of George Armstrong Custer: The True Story of the Battle of Little Bighorn*, 75–76.
5. Monroe County Museum System, Local History Division: Elizabeth Bacon Custer Collection, Frost Collection (Roll 1).
6. Merington, *The Custer Story*, 240–41.
7. Ibid.
8. "The Story of the Calhoun Family & Gen. Armstrong Custer," *Jefferson County Local History*.
9. Pohanka, *A Summer on the Plains*, 116.
10. *True Northerner*, September 27, 1872; Frost, *General Custer's Libbie*, 200.
11. Leckie, *Elizabeth Bacon Custer and the Making of a Myth*, 154; Frost, *General Custer's Libbie*, 202; Pohanka, *A Summer on the Plains*, 106.
12. *Raleigh News*, May 3, 1873.
13. Ibid.
14. Frost, *General Custer's Libbie*, 202–04.
15. Merington, *The Custer Story*, 248–49; Frost, *General Custer's Libbie*, 203–04.
16. Frost, *General Custer's Libbie*, 203–04.
17. Custer, *Boots and Saddles*, 94–95.
18. Ibid.
19. Custer, *Boots and Saddles*, 94–95; *Sioux City Journal*, June 20, 1873; *New Orleans Republican*, June 29, 1873.
20. Frost, *General Custer's Libbie*, 204.
21. Merington, *The Custer Story*, 250.
22. *Bismarck Tribune*, August 27, 1873.
23. Ibid.
24. *Leader Post*, March 20, 1976.
25. Merington, *The Custer Story*, 268–69.
26. Leckie, *Elizabeth Bacon Custer and the Making of a Myth*, 160; *Leader Post*, March 20, 1976; Frost, *General Custer's Libbie*, 214.
27. *Star Tribune*, May 28, 1874.
28. *Boston Globe*, May 4, 1876.
29. Monroe County Museum System, Local History Division: Custer Collection, Frost Collection (Box 2: Files 2-4 and 2-5).
30. Ibid.
31. Ibid.
32. Ibid.

33. Ibid.
34. Ibid.
35. Ibid.
36. *Bismarck Tribune*, May 28, 1877.
37. "Philip Henry Sheridan Papers," *Library of Congress.*
38. Monroe County Museum System, Local History Division: Custer Collection, Frost Collection (Box 2: Files 2-4 and 2-5).
39. Ibid.
40. Ibid.
41. Ibid.
42. Ibid.
43. *Leavenworth Times*, August 1, 1877.
44. Monroe County Museum System, Local History Division: Custer Collection, Frost Collection (Box 2: Files 2-4 and 2-5)
45. *Leavenworth Times*, August 4, 1877.
46. *New York Herald*, August 4, 1877; *Leavenworth Times*, August 4, 1877.
47. Monroe County Museum System, Local History Division: Custer Collection, Frost Collection (Box 2: Files 2-4 and 2-5).
48. Ibid.
49. Ibid.
50. Ibid.

CHAPTER FOUR: THE WIDOWED MOMENT

1. Beinecke Library, Yale University Library, Garrett-Gibson Family Archive, File OCLC Number: 1000592941; "100 Voices: Sioux, Cheyenne, Arapaho, Crow, Arikara, and American Eyewitness Accounts of the Battle of the Little Bighorn," *Astonisher.com.*
2. Willert, "The Wedding Ring of Lieutenant Donald McIntosh: Discovered?" *Research Review Journal of the Little Bighorn Association*, Vol. 10, No. 2, June 1996, 7.
3. Beinecke Library, Yale University Library, Garrett-Gibson Family Archive, File OCLC Number: 1000592941.
4. Beinecke Library, Yale University Library, Garrett-Gibson Family Archive, File OCLC Number: 1000592941; Fougera, *With Custer's Cavalry*, 162–63.
5. Fougera, *With Custer's Cavalry*, 13–14.
6. Thomas, *Canadians with Custer*, 60–64.
7. *Lawrence Tribune*, May 23, 1867; Thomas, *Canadians with Custer*, 65–66.
8. *Richmond Dispatch*, May 8, 1868; Thomas, *Canadians with Custer*, 65–66.
9. Thomas, *Canadians with Custer*, 102–03.
10. Ibid.
11. Fougera, *With Custer's Cavalry*, 74–75.
12. *Leavenworth Times*, August 26, 1870; *Leavenworth Weekly Times*, September 1, 1870.
13. Ibid.
14. Fougera, *With Custer's Cavalry*, 74–76.

15. Beinecke Library, Yale University Library, Garrett-Gibson Family Archive, File OCLC Number: 1000592941.

16. *Nashville Union and American*, April 22, 1873.

17. Beinecke Library, Yale University Library, Garrett-Gibson Family Archive, File OCLC Number: 1000592941; Thomas, *Canadians with Custer*, 123–24; Fougera, *With Custer's Cavalry*, 61–63.

18. Fougera, *With Custer's Cavalry*, 63–68.

19. *Shreveport Journal*, August 22, 1974; *New Orleans Bulletin*, January 28, 1875.

20. Fougera, *With Custer's Cavalry*, 63–68.

21. Beinecke Library, Yale University Library, Garrett-Gibson Family Archive, File OCLC Number: 1000592941.

22. Ibid.

23. Ibid.

24. Ibid.

25. Fougera, *With Custer's Cavalry*, 266–69.

26. Ibid.

27. Ibid.

28. Ibid.

29. Collins, "The Untold Truth of General Custer," *Grunge*.

CHAPTER FIVE: LEFT BEHIND

1. Hanson, *The Conquest of the Missouri*, 175–76.

2. Philbrick, *The Last Stand: Custer, Sitting Bull, and the Battle of the Little Bighorn*, 24–25; Hanson, *The Conquest of the Missouri*, 175–76.

3. Hanson, *The Conquest of the Missouri*, 175–76.

4. Custer, *Boots and Saddles*, 60–61.

5. Frost, *General Custer's Libbie*, 232–33.

6. UC Berkeley Library, Henrietta Smith's Scrapbook (Clippings about Captain Algernon E. Smith, General Custer, the Widows of the Little Bighorn, and the Battle of the Little Bighorn).

7. Ibid.

8. Ibid.

9. *Ellsworth Daily Evening Democrat*, September 12, 1869.

10. Ibid.

11. UC Berkeley Library, Henrietta Smith's Scrapbook; Frost, *General Custer's Libbie*, 197–98.

12. Stiles, *Custer's Trials*, 361–62; Custer, *Tenting on the Plains*, 193–95.

13. Custer, *Tenting on the Plains*, 193–95.

14. Ibid.

15. *Sioux City Journal*, May 4, 1873.

16. Ibid.

17. *Star Tribune*, June 20, 1873.

18. UC Berkeley Library. Henrietta Smith's Scrapbook.

19. Frost, *General Custer's Libbie*, 207–08.

20. Frost, *General Custer's Libbie*, 207–08; Katz, *Custer in Photographs*, 151; UC Berkeley Library, Henrietta Smith's Scrapbook.

21. *Inter Ocean*, July 4, 1874.

22. Ibid.

23. Elizabeth Custer Collection, Chris Kortlander (private collection).

24. UC Berkeley Library, Henrietta Smith's Scrapbook.

25. *Buffalo Weekly Courier*, July 12, 1876.

26. Ibid.

27. Fougera, *With Custer's Cavalry*, 275–76.

28. Elizabeth Custer Collection, Chris Kortlander (private collection); Elizabeth Custer Papers Collection: OGL #1496.

29. *Leavenworth Times*, August 4, 1877.

CHAPTER SIX: ONE SO NOBLE

1. Westcott Family Tree: Westcott Descendants from Stukely and Juliana, Vol. 1; History and Genealogy of the Descendants of Stukely Westcott, Vol. 2; Book of the Appendices of the History and Genealogy of the Ancestors and Some Descendants of Stukely Westcott, 1592–1677 [hereafter, Westcott Family Tree]; UC Berkeley Library, Henrietta Smith's Scrapbook.

2. Westcott Family Tree.

3. UC Berkeley Library, Henrietta Smith's Scrapbook; Westcott Family Tree.

4. Westcott Family Tree.

5. *Daily Kansas Tribune*, September 9, 1869.

6. Ibid.

7. *Yorkville Enquirer*, April 27, 1872; Pearl, "K Troop: The Story of the Eradication of the Original Ku Klux Klan," *Slate*.

8. *Fairfield Herald*, May 31, 1871.

9. Ibid.

10. Westcott Family Tree.

11. *Yorkville Enquirer*, April 27, 1872.

12. *Pittsburgh Weekly Gazette*, April 22, 1872.

13. Elizabeth Custer Collection, Chris Kortlander (private collection); Westcott Family Tree.

14. Custer, *Boots and Saddles*, 30–32; *New Orleans Republican*, June 27, 1873.

15. Elizabeth Custer Collection, Chris Kortlander (private collection); Westcott Family Tree.

16. Elizabeth Custer Collection, Chris Kortlander (private collection); Westcott Family Tree.

17. Custer, *Boots and Saddles*, 80–82.

18. *Boston Post*, February 11, 1874; *Shippensburg News*, February 7, 1874.

19. *Inter Ocean*, July 4, 1874.

20. Pohanka, *A Summer on the Plains*, 110–12.

21. Custer, *Boots and Saddles*, 190.

22. *Chicago Tribune*, July 28, 1874; Custer, *Boots and Saddles*, 196.

23. *St. Louis Dispatch*, August 31, 1874.
24. *Athens Post*, October 2, 1894.
25. *Bismarck Tribune*, December 30, 1874; *Baltimore Sun*, March 29, 1875; *Bismarck Tribune*, June 23, 1875.
26. *Boston Globe*, August 13, 1875.
27. *Mower County Transcript*, October 21, 1875; *Evening Star*, September 14, 1975, *Sacramento Bee*, October 25, 1875.
28. Westcott Family Tree; *Press and Daily Dakotan*, February 18, 1876.
29. *Leavenworth Times*, June 1, 1876.
30. Elizabeth Custer Collection, Chris Kortlander (private collection).
31. Tucker, *Death at the Little Bighorn*, 182–83.
32. Elizabeth Custer Collection, Chris Kortlander (private collection).
33. Ibid.
34. Westcott Family Tree.

CHAPTER SEVEN: DREADFUL DARKNESS

1. Tucker, *Death at the Little Bighorn*, 190–91.
2. Elizabeth Custer Collection, Chris Kortlander (private collection).
3. *Inter Ocean*, July 7, 1876.
4. Cross, *Custer's Lost Officer*, 14–15; "Grace Harrington," *Ancestry.com*; "Henry Harrington," *Ancestry.com*.
5. Cross, *Custer's Lost Officer*, 38–40; *Coldwater Republican*, June 29, 1872.
6. Cross, *Custer's Lost Officer*, 38.
7. *Coldwater Republican*, March 15, 1873.
8. Ibid.
9. *Daily Phoenix*, September 19, 1872; *Raleigh News*, May 3, 1873.
10. *Coldwater Republican*, April 26, 1873.
11. Ibid.
12. Frost, *General Custer's Libbie*, 202–03; *Bangor Daily Whig & Courier*, April 29, 1873.
13. *Coldwater Republican*, July 26, 1873.
14. Ibid.
15. *Coldwater Republican*, August 16, 1873.
16. Ibid.
17. UC Berkeley Library, Henrietta Smith's Scrapbook; Fougera, *With Custer's Cavalry*, 186–88.
18. *Inter Ocean*, July 4, 1874.
19. *Coldwater Republican*, August 8, 1874.
20. Ibid.
21. *Coldwater Republican*, September 19, 1874.
22. Ibid.
23. Cross, *Custer's Lost Officer*, 39–40; *Bismarck Tribune*, March 17, 1875.
24. *Coldwater Republican*, May 29, 1875.
25. Cross, *Custer's Lost Officer*, 62–63; *Coldwater Republican*, March 7, 1876.
26. Cross, *Custer's Lost Officer*, 62–63.

27. *Fall River Daily Evening News,* July 26, 1876.
28. Connell, *Son of the Morning Star: Custer and the Little Bighorn,* 323–25.
29. Elizabeth Custer Collection, Chris Kortlander (private collection).
30. *Buffalo Commercial,* May 15, 1877; *Argus & Patriot,* May 30, 1877.
31. *Evening Gazette,* May 15, 1877.
32. *New Orleans Republican,* May 30, 1877.
33. Elizabeth Custer Collection, Chris Kortlander (private collection).

CHAPTER EIGHT: ALONE IN THE SHADOWS

1. Elizabeth Custer Collection, Chris Kortlander (private collection); Custer, *Boots and Saddles,* 222.
2. Frost, *General Custer's Libbie,* 230–31.
3. Ibid., 219, 233–34.
4. Ibid.
5. Elizabeth Custer Collection, Chris Kortlander (private collection).
6. Donovan, *Custer and the Little Bighorn,* 194.
7. Forsyth, *The Story of the Soldier,* 328.
8. McClellan, *McClellan's Own Story,* 365–66.
9. Thomas Weir Military Records & Personal Letters, 1863–1876.
10. Elizabeth Custer Collection, Chris Kortlander (private collection).
11. Frost, *General Custer's Libbie,* 233.
12. Elizabeth Custer Collection, Chris Kortlander (private collection).
13. Ibid.
14. Ladenheim, *Custer's Thorn,* 198; Frost, *General Custer's Libbie,* 238–39.
15. Elizabeth Custer Collection, Chris Kortlander (private collection).
16. Frost, *General Custer's Libbie,* 237–38; Elizabeth Custer Collection, Chris Kortlander (private collection).
17. Frost, *General Custer's Libbie,* 240; Merington, *The Custer Story,* 285.
18. Elizabeth Custer Collection, Chris Kortlander (private collection); Frost, *General Custer's Libbie,* 223; Merington, *The Custer Story,* 285.
19. Elizabeth Custer Collection, Chris Kortlander (private collection).
20. Ibid.
21. Ibid.
22. Ibid.
23. Ibid.
24. Reece, "Interment of the Custer Dead," *Friends of the Little Bighorn Battlefield.*
25. Ibid.
26. Ibid.
27. Frost, *General Custer's Libbie,* 240–42.
28. *Brooklyn Daily Eagle,* October 11, 1877.
29. Ibid.
30. Ibid.
31. Elizabeth Custer Collection, Chris Kortlander (private collection).
32. Ibid.

33. Ibid.
34. Ibid.
35. Frost, *General Custer's Libbie*, 223.
36. *San Francisco Chronicle*, December 22, 1886.
37. Ibid.
38. Hoagland, *Lawrence Park: Bronxville's Turn-of-the-Century Art Colony*, 66–68.
39. *New York Times*, November 7, 1886.
40. Elizabeth Custer Collection, Chris Kortlander (private collection).
41. UC Berkeley Library, Henrietta Smith's Scrapbook.
42. Ibid.
43. Ibid.
44. Frost, *General Custer's Libbie*, 246–47.
45. Ibid.
46. Elizabeth Custer Collection, Chris Kortlander (private collection).
47. Ibid.
48. Ibid.
49. Ibid.
50. Ibid.

Chapter Nine: Broken Souls

1. *St. Louis Republican*, July 7, 1876.
2. Ibid.
3. Ibid.
4. UC Berkeley Library, Henrietta Smith's Scrapbook.
5. Ibid.
6. Ibid.
7. *New York Herald*, July 20, 1876.
8. *London Saturday Review*, August 2, 1876.
9. Ibid.
10. UC Berkeley Library, Henrietta Smith's Scrapbook.
11. *Army and Navy Journal: Gazette of the Regular and Volunteer Forces*, October 23, 1876.
12. Ibid.
13. Ibid.
14. UC Berkeley Library, Henrietta Smith's Scrapbook; Frost, *General Custer's Libbie*, 233.
15. UC Berkeley Library, Henrietta Smith's Scrapbook.
16. Ibid.
17. Ibid.
18. Ibid.
19. *Altoona Tribune*, March 8, 1888; House Report No. 2520, 50th Congress, 1st Session, 1888.
20. Pohanka, *A Summer on the Plains*, 128–29.
21. *Carlisle Weekly Herald*, October 6, 1881.

22. Pohanka, *A Summer on the Plains*, 128–29.
23. *Carlisle Evening Herald*, August 24, 1907.
24. Pohanka, *A Summer on the Plains*, 128–29; *The Sentinel*, July 17, 1896.
25. *The Sentinel*, December 10, 1914.
26. Ibid.
27. *The Sentinel*, December 10, 1914; *Harrisburg Daily Independent*, December 11, 1914.
28. *Star Tribune*, January 17, 1882; *Detroit Free Press*, November 4, 1883; *The Lance*, February 2, 1884.
29. *Carlisle Weekly Herald*, October 17, 1888.
30. Ibid.
31. *Wilson County Citizen*, November 13, 1885; *Detroit Free Press*, February 22, 1891.
32. Elizabeth Custer Collection, Chris Kortlander (private collection).
33. *Morning Journal Courier*, February 22, 1898; *Idaho County Free Press*, February 5, 1897.
34. *Brooklyn Times Union*, February 24, 1900.
35. *Times Herald*, July 8, 1903; *New York Tribune*, March 23, 1910.
36. *St. Joseph News Press*, March 23, 1910.
37. Fougera, *With Custer's Cavalry*, 279–80.
38. Ibid.
39. Ibid.
40. Willert, "The Wedding Ring of Lieutenant Donald McIntosh: Discovered?" 7.
41. UC Berkeley Library, Henrietta Smith's Scrapbook.
42. Ibid.
43. *Pittsburgh Press*, August 14, 1903.
44. Westcott Family Tree.
45. *Berkeley Daily Gazette*, May 1, 1903.
46. Ibid.
47. *San Jose Mercury News*, December 15, 1915.
48. *Chattanooga Commercial*, December 10, 1887.
49. *Buffalo Evening News*, December 3, 1887.
50. *Coldwater Republican*, August 26, 1885; *Coldwater Republican*, July 11, 1885.
51. *Coldwater Republican*, May 4, 1886.
52. *Buffalo Evening News*, December 3, 1887; *Chattanooga Commercial*, December 10, 1887.
53. *Chattanooga Commercial*, December 10, 1887.
54. Ibid.
55. Ibid.
56. Ibid.
57. Ibid.

Chapter Ten: Last to Go

1. *Frontier Fighters*, June 26, 1926.
2. Custer, *Boots and Saddles*, 222.
3. Elizabeth Custer Collection, Chris Kortlander (private collection).

4. Ibid.
5. Ibid.
6. Ibid.
7. Ibid.
8. Ibid.
9. *Billings Gazette*, June 13, 1921.
10. Ibid.
11. Frost, *General Custer's Libbie*, 314–15; *Brooklyn Daily Eagle*, June 8, 1922; "Pottery Online Resources," *Greenwich House*.
12. *Standard Union*, November 9, 1928.
13. Ibid.
14. Ibid.
15. *Daily Press*, June 30, 1929.
16. Ibid.
17. *New York Times*, June 25, 1931.
18. *Salt Lake Tribune*, April 16, 1933.
19. *San Antonio Express*, April 11, 1933.
20. *Billings Gazette*, April 5, 1933.
21. *Atlanta Journal*, May 24, 1897; Ladenheim, *Custer's Thorn*, 269.
22. *Salt Lake Tribune*, May 12, 1933.
23. Ibid.
24. *New York Herald*, June 25, 1926.

Bibliography

Books

Barnett, Louise. *Touched by Fire: The Life, Death, and Mythic Afterlife of George Armstrong Custer.* Lincoln: University of Nebraska Press, 2006.

Connell, Evan S. *Son of the Morning Star: Custer and the Little Bighorn.* New York: North Point Press, 1997.

Cross, Walt. *Custer's Lost Officer: The Search for Lieutenant Henry Moore Harrington, 7th U.S. Cavalry.* Stillwater, OK: Cross Publications, 2006.

Custer, Elizabeth. *Boots and Saddles, or Life in Dakota with General Custer.* Norman: University of Oklahoma Press, 1961.

———. *Tenting on the Plains.* New York: Charles L. Webster & Co., 1889.

Donovan, Jim. *Custer and the Little Bighorn.* Stillwater, MN: Voyageur Press, Inc., 2001.

Forsyth, G. A. *The Story of the Soldier.* New York: D. Appleton & Company, 1900.

Fougera, Katherine Gibson. *With Custer's Cavalry.* Caldwell, ID: Caxton Press, 1940.

Frost, Lawrence A. *General Custer's Libbie.* Seattle, WA: Superior Publishing Company, 1976.

Hanson, Joseph Mills. *The Conquest of the Missouri: Grant Marsh, Custer, and the 1876 Campaign.* Independently published, 2019.

Hatch, Thom. *The Last Days of George Armstrong Custer: The True Story of the Battle of the Little Bighorn.* New York: St. Martin's Press, 2015.

Hoagland, Loretta. *Lawrence Park: Bronxville's Turn-of-the-Century Art Colony.* Bronxville, NY: Lawrence Park Hilltop Association, 1992.

Johnson, Virginia Weisel. *The Unregimented General: A Biography of Nelson A. Miles.* Whitefish, MT: Literary Licensing, LLC, 2011.

Katz, D. Mark. *Custer in Photographs: A Photographic Biography of America's Most Intriguing Boy General.* Garryowen, MT: Custer Battlefield Museum Publishing, 2001.

Kazanjian, Howard, and Chris Enss. *None Wounded, None Missing, All Dead: The Story of Elizabeth Bacon Custer.* Guilford, CT: TwoDot Books, 2011.

Ladenheim, J. C. *Custer's Thorn: The Life of Frederick W. Benteen.* Westminster, MA: Heritage Books, 2007.

Leckie, Shirley. *Elizabeth Bacon Custer and the Making of a Myth.* Norman: University of Oklahoma Press, 1993.

Leighton, Margaret. *The Story of General Custer.* New York: Grosset & Dunlap, 1954.

McClellan, George B. *McClellan's Own Story*. London, England: Sampson Low, Marston, Searle & Riverton, 1887.

Merington, Marguerite. *The Custer Story: The Life and Intimate Letters of General George A. Custer and His Wife Elizabeth*. Lincoln: University of Nebraska Press, 1950.

Monaghan, Jay. *Custer: The Life of General George Armstrong Custer*. Lincoln: University of Nebraska Press, 1959.

Philbrick, Nathaniel. *The Last Stand: Custer, Sitting Bull, and the Battle of the Little Bighorn*. New York: Viking Penguin, 2011.

Pohanka, Brian C. *A Summer on the Plains with Custer's 7th Cavalry: The 1870 Diary of Annie Gibson Roberts*. Lynchburg, VA: Schroeder Publications, 2004.

Poolman, Jeremy. *A Wounded Thing Must Hide: In Search of Libbie Custer*. New York: Bloomsbury, 2002.

Schneider, George. *The Freeman Journal*. San Rafael, CA: Presidio Press, 1977.

Stiles, T. J. *Custer's Trials: A Life on the Frontier of a New America*. New York: Vintage, 2016.

Thomas, Mary. *Canadians with Custer*. Ontario, Canada: Dundurn Press, 2012.

Tucker, Phillip Thomas. *Death at the Little Bighorn: A New Look at Custer, His Tactics, and the Tragic Decisions Made at the Last Stand*. New York: Skyhorse, 2017.

HISTORICAL ARCHIVES MATERIAL

Beinecke Rare Book & Manuscript Library, Yale University Library, Garrett-Gibson Family, OCLC Number: 10000592941.

Elizabeth Custer Collection, Chris Kortlander (private collection).

Elizabeth Custer Paper Collection: OGL #1496. Elwyn B. Robinson Department of Special Collections, Chester Fritz Library, University of North Dakota.

Highland Falls Historical Society, Hanging File on Harrington Family entitled "The News of the Highlands, July 30, 1892."

House Report No. 2520, 50th Congress, 1st Session, 1888.

Monroe County Museum System, Local History Division: Custer Collection, Frost Collection (Box 2: Files 2-4 and 2-5).

———. Elizabeth Bacon Custer Collection, Frost Collection (Box 1, Folder 15).

———. Elizabeth Bacon Custer Collection, Frost Collection (Roll 1).

Thomas Weir Military Records & Personal Letters, 1863–1876 (National Archives and Records Administration, M1064C:492).

UC Berkeley Library, Henrietta Smith's Scrapbook (Clippings about Captain Algernon E. Smith, General Custer, the Widows of the Little Bighorn, and the Battle of the Little Bighorn).

The Westcott Family Tree: Westcott Descendants from Stukely and Juliana, Vol. 1; History and Genealogy of the Descendants of Stukely Westcott, Vol. 2; Book of the Appendices of the History and Genealogy of the Ancestors and Some Descendants of Stukely Westcott, 1592–1677.

MAGAZINES AND PAMPHLETS

Clarke, Sarah. "The Hope Pioneer (Hope, North Dakota): The Brave Mrs. Custer," December 15, 1910.

Evans-Hatch, Gail. *Centuries Along the Upper Niobrara: Historic Resource Study: Agate Fossil Beds National Monument Nebraska.* National Park Service Publication, 2008.

"General Custer's Sister Passes Away," *Sacramento Union,* Vol. 119, No. 31, March 24, 1910.

Parmalee, Mary Manley. "A Child's Recollection of the Summer of '76, Nebraska Territory." Edited by Herbert Coffeen. *Tepee Book 1* (June 1916).

US Army & Navy Journal & Gazette (New York, New York), July 15, 1876.

———. October 23, 1876.

Willert, James. "The Wedding Ring of Lieutenant Donald McIntosh: Discovered?" *Research Review Journal of the Little Bighorn Association,* Vol. 10, No. 2, June 1996, 7.

NEWSPAPERS

Altoona Tribune (Altoona, Pennsylvania), March 8, 1888.

Argus & Patriot (Montpelier, Vermont), May 30, 1877.

Army and Navy Journal: Gazette of the Regular and Volunteer Forces (New York, New York), October 23, 1876.

Athens Post (Athens, Tennessee), October 21, 1894.

Atlanta Journal (Atlanta, Georgia), May 24, 1897.

Baltimore Sun (Baltimore, Maryland), March 29, 1875.

Bangor Daily Whig & Courier (Bangor, Maine), April 29, 1873.

Beemer Times (Beemer, Nebraska), December 26, 1940.

Beloit Gazette (Beloit, Kansas), June 9, 1877.

Berkeley Daily Gazette (Berkeley, California), May 1, 1903.

Billings Gazette (Billings, Montana), June 13, 1921.

———. November 13, 1932.

———. April 5, 1933.

Bismarck Tribune (Bismarck, North Dakota), August 27, 1873.

———. December 30, 1874.

———. March 17, 1875.

———. June 23, 1875.

Bismarck Weekly Tribune (Bismarck, North Dakota), May 24, 1876.

———. August 24, 1876.

Boston Globe (Boston, Massachusetts), July 14, 1873.

———. August 13, 1875.

———. May 4, 1876.

Boston Post (Boston, Massachusetts), February 11, 1874.

Brooklyn Daily Eagle (Brooklyn, New York), October 11, 1877.

———. June 8, 1922.

———. June 8, 1924.

Brooklyn Times Union (Brooklyn, New York), February 24, 1900.

Buffalo Commercial (Buffalo, New York), May 15, 1877.
Buffalo Evening News (Buffalo, New York), December 3, 1887.
Buffalo Weekly Courier (Buffalo, New York), July 12, 1876.
Burlington Daily Sentinel (Burlington, Vermont), August 15, 1876.
Canton Independent-Sentinel (Canton, Pennsylvania), December 9, 1887.
Carlisle Evening Herald (Carlisle, Pennsylvania), August 24, 1907.
Carlisle Weekly Herald (Carlisle, Pennsylvania), October 6, 1881.
———. October 17, 1888.
Chattanooga Commercial (Chattanooga, Tennessee), December 10, 1887.
Chicago Tribune (Chicago, Illinois), July 28, 1874.
Coldwater Republican (Coldwater, Michigan), June 29, 1872.
———. March 15, 1873.
———. April 26, 1873.
———. July 26, 1873.
———. August 8, 1874.
———. September 19, 1874.
———. May 29, 1875.
———. March 7, 1876.
———. June 26, 1885.
———. July 11, 1885.
———. May 4, 1886.
Daily Gazette (Wilmington, Delaware), September 19, 1876.
Daily Kansas Tribune (Lawrence, Kansas), September 9, 1869.
Daily Memphis Avalanche (Memphis, Tennessee), April 29, 1873.
Daily Phoenix (Columbia, South Carolina), September 19, 1872.
Daily Press (Newport News, Virginia), June 30, 1929.
Daily Record of the Times (Wilkes-Barre, Pennsylvania), July 16, 1876.
Democrat and Chronicle (Rochester, New York), July 15, 1876.
———. July 20, 1876.
Detroit Free Press (Detroit, Michigan), August 11, 1874.
———. November 4, 1883.
———. February 22, 1891.
Ellsworth Daily Evening Democrat (Ellsworth, Maine), September 12, 1869.
Evening Gazette (Port Jervis, New York), May 15, 1877.
Evening News (San Jose, California), December 15, 1915.
Evening Star (Washington, DC), September 14, 1975.
Fairfield Herald (Winnsboro, South Carolina), May 31, 1871.
Fall River Daily Evening News (Fall River, Massachusetts), July 26, 1876.
Fargo Record (Fargo, North Dakota), August 4, 1895.
Findlay Jeffersonian (Findlay, Ohio), August 4, 1876.
Galveston Daily News (Galveston, Texas), December 22, 1874.
Harrisburg Daily Independent (Harrisburg, Pennsylvania), December 11, 1914.
Helena Weekly Herald (Helena, Montana), September 11, 1873.
Idaho County Free Press (Grangeville, Idaho), February 5, 1897.

Inter Ocean (Chicago, Illinois), July 4, 1874.
————. July 7, 1876.
Interior Journal (Stanford, Kentucky), May 5, 1885.
Junction City Weekly (Junction City, Kansas), August 5, 1876.
Knoxville Daily Tribune (Knoxville, Tennessee), July 15, 1882.
Lamoille Newsdealer (Hyde Park, Vermont), December 23, 1874.
Lancaster Examiner and Herald (Lancaster, Pennsylvania), July 19, 1876.
The Lance (Topeka, Kansas), February 2, 1884.
Lawrence Tribune (Lawrence, Kansas), May 23, 1867.
Leader-Post (Regina, Saskatchewan, Canada), March 20, 1976.
Leavenworth Times (Leavenworth, Kansas), June 1, 1876.
————. August 1, 1877.
————. August 4, 1877.
————. August 26, 1870.
Leavenworth Weekly Times (Leavenworth, Kansas), September 1, 1870.
London Saturday Review (London, England), August 2, 1876.
Los Angeles Express (Los Angeles, California), December 15, 1915.
Macon Telegraph (Macon, Georgia), February 8, 1886.
Mendocino Beacon (Mendocino, California), June 26, 1915.
The Missoulian (Missoula, Montana), May 26, 1984.
Monroe Commercial (Monroe, Michigan), August 13, 1876.
Morning Journal Courier (New Haven, Connecticut), February 22, 1898.
Mower County Transcript (Austin, Minnesota), October 12, 1875.
Nashville Union and American (Nashville, Tennessee), February 21, 1873.
————. April 22, 1873.
National Republican (Washington, DC), October 4, 1865.
————. March 3, 1874.
New North-West (Deer Lodge, Montana), April 21, 1876.
New Orleans Bulletin (New Orleans, Louisiana), January 1, 1875.
————. January 28, 1875.
New Orleans Republican (New Orleans, Louisiana), June 27, 1873.
————. June 29, 1873.
————. July 16, 1876.
————. May 30, 1877.
New York Daily Herald (New York, New York), August 4, 1877.
New York Herald (New York, New York), July 17, 1876.
————. July 20, 1876.
————. June 25, 1926.
New York Times (New York, New York), November 7, 1886.
————. June 25, 1931.
New-York Tribune (New York, New York), March 23, 1910.
Philadelphia Inquirer (Philadelphia, Pennsylvania), February 12, 1880.
Pittsburgh Daily Post (Pittsburgh, Pennsylvania), May 14, 1874.
————. December 11, 1914.

Pittsburgh Press (Pittsburgh, Pennsylvania), August 4, 1903.
Pittsburgh Weekly Gazette (Pittsburgh, Pennsylvania), April 22, 1872.
Press and Daily Dakotan (Yankton, South Dakota), February 18, 1876.
———. April 29, 1876.
Raleigh News (Raleigh, North Carolina), May 3, 1873.
Richmond Dispatch (Richmond, Virginia), May 8, 1868.
———. September 18, 1876.
Sacramento Bee (Sacramento, California), October 25, 1875.
St. Joseph News-Press Gazette (St. Joseph, Missouri), March 23, 1910.
St. Louis Dispatch (St. Louis, Missouri), August 31, 1874.
St. Louis Republican (St. Louis, Missouri), July 7, 1876.
St. Paul Tribune (St. Paul, Minnesota), April 21, 1876.
Salt Lake Tribune (Salt Lake City, Utah), April 16, 1933.
———. May 12, 1933.
San Antonio Express (San Antonio, Texas), April 11, 1933.
San Francisco Chronicle (San Francisco, California), December 22, 1886.
San Jose Mercury News (San Jose, California), December 13, 1915.
The Sentinel (Carlisle, Pennsylvania), July 17, 1896.
———. December 10, 1914.
Shippensburg News (Shippensburg, Pennsylvania), February 7, 1874.
Shreveport Journal (Shreveport, Louisiana), August 22, 1974.
Sioux City Journal (Sioux City, Iowa), May 4, 1873.
———. June 20, 1873.
Standard Union (Brooklyn, New York), June 8, 1924.
———. November 9, 1928.
Star Tribune (Minneapolis, Minnesota), June 20, 1873.
———. May 28, 1874.
———. August 14, 1876.
———. January 17, 1882.
Times Herald (Port Huron, Michigan), July 8, 1903.
True Northerner (Paw Paw, Michigan), September 27, 1872.
Tyrone Daily Herald (Tyrone, Pennsylvania), December 5, 1887.
Wheeling Daily Intelligencer (Wheeling, West Virginia), August 9, 1876.
Wilson County Citizen (Fredonia, Kansas), November 13, 1885.
Yates Center News (Yates Center, Kansas), June 29, 1877.
Yorkville Enquirer (York, South Carolina), April 27, 1872.

WEBSITES
Calhoun, James. *Ancestry.com.*
Collins, Jan Mackell. "The Untold Truth of General Custer," *Grunge,* https://www
    .grunge.com/216849/the-untold-truth-of-general-custer/.
"Grace. H. Harrington." *Ancestry.com.*
"Henry Harrington." *Ancestry.com.*

"Libbie Custer Makes a Secret Plea to Aid the Widows of Captain Yates, Lt. Calhoun, and Enlisted Men," *Shapell*, https://www.shapell.org/manuscript/libbie-custer-solicit-army-funds-for-little-bighorn-widows.

"Lieutenant McIntosh's Wedding Ring," *Heritage Auctions*, https://historical.ha.com/itm/military-and-patriotic/indian-wars/lieutenant-mcintosh-s-wedding-ring-a-poignant-souvenir/a/6197-49065.s.

"100 Voices: Sioux, Cheyenne, Arapaho, Crow, Arikara, and American Eyewitness Accounts of the Battle of the Little Bighorn," *Astonisher.com*, https://www.astonisher.com/archives/museum/index_never_found.html.

Pearl, Matthew. "K Troop: The Story of the Eradication of the Original Ku Klux Klan, *Slate*, http://www.slate.com/articles/news_and_politics/history/2016/03/how_a_detachment_of_u_s_army_soldiers_smoked_out_the_original_ku_klux_klan.html.

"Philip Henry Sheridan Papers," *Library of Congress*, https://www.loc.gov/collections/philip-henry-sheridan-papers.

"Pottery Online Resources," *Greenwich House*, https://www.greenwichhouse.org/pottery-about/online-resources.

Reece, Bob. "Interment of the Custer Dead," *Friends of the Little Bighorn Battlefield*, https://www.friendslittlebighorn.com/dusttodust.htm.

Smith, Henrietta. *Ancestry.com*.

"Standard Atlas of Holmes County, Ohio," *Ohio Memory Collection*, https://www.ohiomemory.org/digital/collection/p267401coll36/id/26796/rec/2.

"The Story of the Calhoun Family & Gen. Armstrong Custer," *Jefferson County Local History*, https://www.jeffersoncountylocalhistory.org/milcalhounfamily.

"Victorian Days: Death and Mourning," *AVictorian.com*, http://www.angelpig.net/victorian/mourning.html.

INDEX

Note: Page numbers in bold indicate photographs or illustrations.

About the Authors

Chris Enss is a *New York Times* best-selling author who has been writing about women of the Old West for more than twenty years. She has penned more than forty published books on the subject. Her work has been honored with five Will Rogers Medallion Awards, two Elmer Kelton Book Awards, an Oklahoma Center for the Book Award, and was a Western Writers of America Spur Award Finalist. Her books *Thunder Over the Prairie*, *The Death Row All Stars*, and *The Trials of Annie Oakley* have been optioned by major production companies for feature films. Enss's most recent works are *According to Kate: The Legendary Life of Big Nose Kate, Love of Doc Holliday*; *No Place for a Woman: The Struggle for Suffrage in the Wild West*; and *Iron Women: The Ladies Who Helped Build the Railroad*.

Enss is the current president of Western Writers of America, serves as executive director of the Will Rogers Medallion Award, and is a licensed private investigator.

Howard Kazanjian is an award-winning producer and entertainment executive who has been producing feature films and television programs for more than twenty-five years. He lives in San Marino, California.

Chris Kortlander has been a Western Americana collector and dealer for most of his adult life. His personal collection was assembled over several decades and features some of the rarest and most desirable works and historic collectibles in the province of the Indian Wars and America's westward expansion. Kortlander's appreciation for the unique history and grandeur of the West goes far beyond building his own amazing personal collection of books, manuscripts, and Western Americana collectibles. In addition, he has published *Custer in Photographs* and produced a play, *Libbie*, which offers a new take on the Battle of the Little Bighorn and its aftermath.